AF560408

Geronimo Stilton

THE TREASURES OF THE KINGOM

THE SIXTEENTH ADVENTURE IN THE KINGDOM OF FANTASY

Scholastic Inc.

Copyright © 2022 by Mondadori Libri S.p.A for PIEMME, Italy. International Rights © Atlantyca S.p.A., Via Leopardi 8, 20123 Milan, Italy; foreignrights@atlantyca.it, atlantyca.com. English translation © 2023 by Atlantyca S.p.A.

The publisher does not have any control over and does not assume any responsibility for author or third-party websites or their content.

GERONIMO STILTON names, characters, and related indicia are copyright, trademark, and exclusive license of Atlantyca S.p.A. All rights reserved. The moral right of the author has been asserted. Based on an original idea by Elisabetta Dami. geronimostilton.com.

Published by Scholastic Inc., *Publishers since 1920*, 557 Broadway, New York, NY 10012. SCHOLASTIC and associated logos are trademarks and/or registered trademarks of Scholastic Inc.

Stilton is the name of a famous English cheese. It is a registered trademark of the Stilton Cheesemakers' Association. For more information, go to stiltoncheese .co.uk

No part of this publication may be reproduced, stored in a retrieval system, or transmitted in any form or by any means, electronic, mechanical, photocopying, recording, or otherwise, without written permission of the copyright holder. For information regarding permission, please contact: Atlantyca S.p.A.

This book is a work of fiction. Names, characters, places, and incidents are either the product of the author's imagination or are used fictitiously, and any resemblance to actual persons, living or dead, business establishments, events, or locales is entirely coincidental.

Library of Congress Cataloging-in-Publication Data available

ISBN 978-93-5471-649-2

Text by Geronimo Stilton
Original title *Il Meraviglioso libro dei libri*
Cover by Danilo Barozzi
Art Director: Iacopo Bruno
Illustrations Carla Debernardi, Silvia Bigolin, and Andrea Alba Benelle
Graphics by Federica Fontana

Special thanks to Shannon Decker

Translated by Julia Heim

Interior design by Becky James

Printed in India at : VK Global Digital Private Limited

First Edition, November 2023

This reprint edition, August 2025

Little Owl Feathers?

It was a beautiful spring morning in New Mouse City, and I woke up full of **energy**. I just knew that it was going to be a fabumouse day!

I poked my head out the window. A light breeze caressed my snout . . . and then a tuft of feathers as soft as snow fell onto my nose! Holey cheese!

Shoop,
shoop,
shoop!

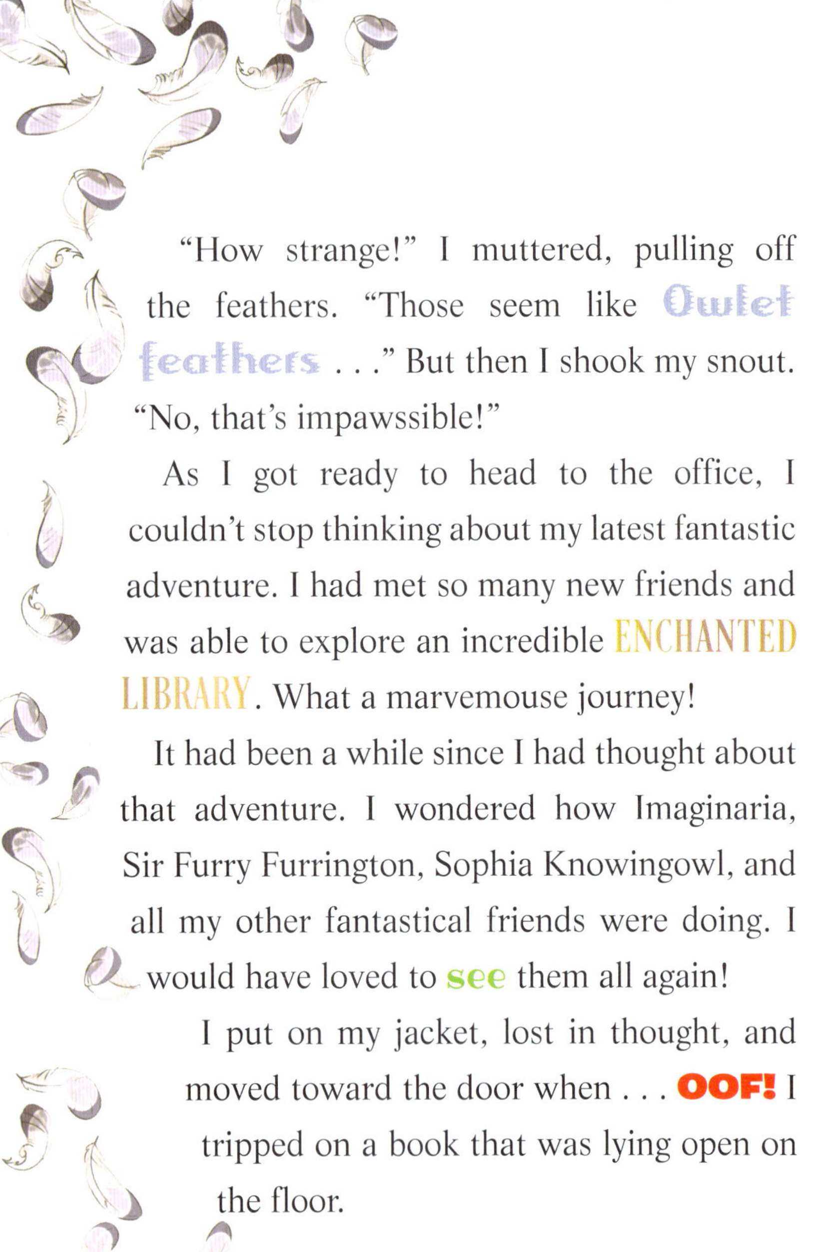

"How strange!" I muttered, pulling off the feathers. "Those seem like **Owlet feathers** . . ." But then I shook my snout. "No, that's impawssible!"

As I got ready to head to the office, I couldn't stop thinking about my latest fantastic adventure. I had met so many new friends and was able to explore an incredible ENCHANTED LIBRARY. What a marvemouse journey!

It had been a while since I had thought about that adventure. I wondered how Imaginaria, Sir Furry Furrington, Sophia Knowingowl, and all my other fantastical friends were doing. I would have loved to **see** them all again!

I put on my jacket, lost in thought, and moved toward the door when . . . **OOF!** I tripped on a book that was lying open on the floor.

"How strange!" I whispered. "I don't remember leaving that there last night. I was reading a totally different **BOOK**!" I picked it up and took a better look. "Cheese and crackers, what a coincidence. This is the story that I wrote about my fantastic adventure with

Imaginaria!"

I began to leaf through it. **PUFF!** Another feather appeared from between the pages! How did that get there?

I shrugged and turned my snout back to the **BOOK**. Memories washed over me as I read about the incredible voyage that led to my new title:

THE FANTASTIC HERO!

Everything You Need to Know About My Fantastic Adventure

Everything started the day that I, Geronimo Stilton, editor of *The Rodent's Gazette*, found myself inside the **ENCHANTED LIBRARY**. It was a magical place, but it looked like an abandoned building in **Singing Stone Plaza** to the rodents of New Mouse City. It was there that I met Imaginaria; her **helpers**, Furry and Sophia; and their loyal friends, the thirty-three Owlets.

A magical place where all possible (and impossible) books that have been written (and will never, ever be written) are held.

According to Imaginaria, I was the **FANTASTIC HERO** they were looking for! Imaginaria needed a hero because she was in trouble . . .

Imaginaria

Furry

The Owlets

Sophia

big trouble. Regulus, the mysterious wicked wizard, had put a spell on her. Only I could save her by writing a **fantastic** story full of inspiration!

Luckily, thanks to my team of fantastic friends, I succeeded. I even ended up turning Regulus to lead! He was transformed into a statue that Imaginaria placed at the center of **Singing Stone Plaza**.

On top of all that, I came home with three fabumouse things: the fantastic pen (which is just my usual pen with some extra oomph!), my fantastic portrait, and the Golden Library Card.

I smiled at the memory, but I had started to feel a bit unsettled. First, I'd seen all those feathers, then my book had ended up on the floor right by the door so that I tripped on it. Could Imaginaria be trying to get my attention?

Just then the book's pages began to turn — all on their own! Squeak, what was happening?! Suddenly, the pages stopped and I jumped in surprise. The open pages were completely BLANK! It was as if the ink had disappeared.

Whaaaat?!

I checked again, my paws shaking. Sure enough, from pages fifty-seven to sixty, all the text was gone!

"How can that be?" I squeaked out loud to myself. "Well, that was probably a defective copy . . . even though the last time I LEAFED through it, everything seemed normal."

I flipped and flipped the pages with my paws, thinking hard. Then I gave up. "I'm going to be late! I have to go. I'll deal with this tonight."

I felt an anxiousness churning in my stomach, so before I left I turned around and went over to my desk. I opened the drawer to look for the Golden Library Card that Imaginaria had given me. It gave me access to the Enchanted Library whenever I wanted. It was there, safe and secure, looking like a regular old library card. Whew!

"What a 'fraidy mouse!" I said with a little laugh. "If **something** had happened to Imaginaria or the Enchanted Library, I would already know."

But just in case, I took the Golden Library Card and put it in my pocket.

As I walked through the streets of New Mouse

City, I continued to search for ***fantastic signs***. Maybe an elf hanging from a tree branch in the park? Or a streak in the sky left by a witchcat? Or the windows of a house that had transformed into eyes? **But I didn't see anything!**

Everything was normal in New Mouse City. Cheesy creampuffs, I was worrying for nothing! So, when I finally arrived at *The Rodent's Gazette* offices, I said hello to everyone and got ready to bury my snout in work.

I sat down and glanced at the portrait of me on my desk. **I turned as pale as a ball of mozzarella!**

This wasn't just any portrait; it was the **fantastic portrait** that Imaginaria had given me as a thank-you gift for saving her. In the image,

I had a proud and determined look on my snout, like a true hero! But now . . .

"Squeak!" I exclaimed. "Why does my portrait look so **SAD**?"

Singing Stone Plaza

I began to think about what might have happened: first the feathers, then Imaginaria's book with all those blank pages, and now the fantastic portrait. Something really **STRANGE** was going on!

I turned to the portrait, hoping that it could give me answers. "There must be a good reason for all of this," I muttered. "Something that explains everything."

A chill ran down my fur from snout to tail. "No, **someone**! That terrible wizard must be behind this! That whisker-trembling terror!

THE WICKED REGULUS!"

Squeak, I had better check on the ***fantastic pen***! I started looking for it everywhere: in my pen holder, in my desk drawers, under piles of paper . . .

I turned to the portrait again and exclaimed, "I can't find it! Why am I so disorganized?"

A voice answered me. "Uh-oh, Cousin, are you getting mad at a picture now, you cheesebrain? It can't hear you!"

I turned with a start. It was my cousin Trap. Of course he had caught me squeaking to myself!

I sighed, **embarrassed**. "Umm, no — I mean, yes. Every once in a while I talk to the portrait, and it helps me get my ideas straight. I'm a bit worried and —"

My cousin put a firm paw on my shoulder. "**WORRIED?** Right. Me, too!"

My jaw dropped in surprise. "What? Why?"

He threw his paws in the air. "I'm worried because I'm launching my new **BUSINESS** as a door-to-door rebel appliance tamer, and I need some publicity!"

I was shocked. "What are you talking about?"

He puffed out his chest proudly. "Dishwasher not responding to your commands? Is your computer shutting down when you need it most? Does your photocopier have a life of its own? Never fear, Trap is here!"

As he spoke, I saw a bunch of **feathers**

blow in through the window. For the love of cheese, more feathers?

I pointed them out to my cousin. "You know, I have something urgent to do. Those feathers —"

Trap looked me up and down suspiciously. "**Feathers?** I don't see any feathers! Are you making up excuses? You don't want to help your dear cousin with a bit of advertising? After all I have done for you!"

I pointed a paw. ***"You don't see the feathers?"***

Trap rolled his eyes. "No, of course not, Gerrykins! Next time, find a better excuse to get rid of me!" He stormed out of my office just as fast as he'd arrived.

Crusty cat litter! I followed Trap, ready to tell him that I would help. As I did, the feathers flew over

the papers on my desk, uncovering the

fantastic pen!

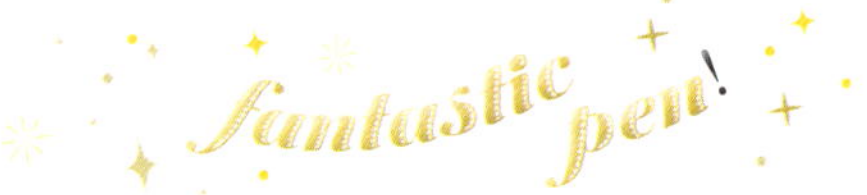

But I didn't see it, and I closed the door behind me. I tried to catch up to Trap, but the feathers **pushed** me toward the exit. Cheese and crackers, what was happening? All I could do

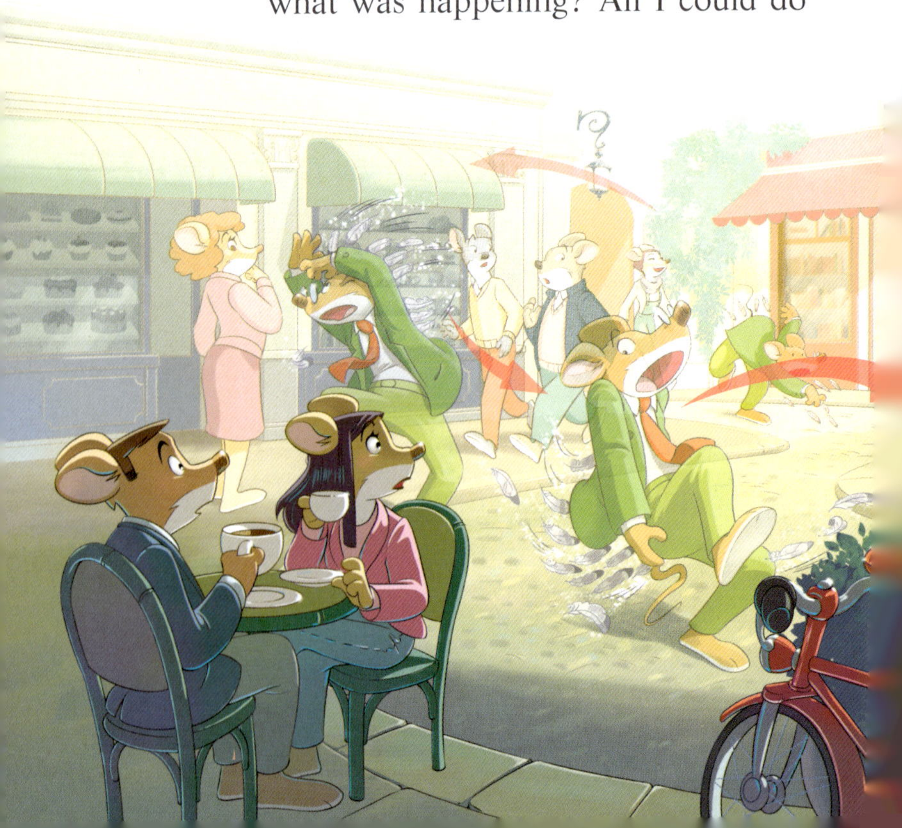

was send my cousin a text: "Don't worry, I promise I'll lend you a paw. But first there's something I have to do!"

I twisted my tail into knots.

Something wasn't right!

I walked through the city, still followed by the feathers . . .

The feathers surely belonged to the Owlets! But where had all the **Owlets** ended up? What did they need from me? What did I have to do?

I continued to walk aimlessly, always followed by feathers. They **poked** my undertail, tickled my whiskers, and pulled at my jacket. Rodents on the street looked at me, shaking their snouts. No one else could see the feathers, so I must have looked like a total cheesebrain!

Suddenly, they all formed a giant flying arrow that pointed north!

"Squeak!" I exclaimed. "Silly me! That's the way to Singing Stone Plaza."

I ran as fast as my paws would take me, my **heart** beating faster and faster. I was scared of what I would find at Singing Stone Plaza . . . or what I wouldn't find.

When I arrived at the center of the square, I knew for sure that something was unsqueakably wrong.

The statue of Regulus had disappeared!

Dear readers, I was so worried. Regulus had disappeared! That could only mean one

thing: Imaginaria was in DANGER! And so were the rest of us. Suddenly, I began to shiver.

I was really shaken. I was pawsitively trembling!

But wait — it was actually the Golden Library Card that was vibrating in my pocket. It was shaking everything!

The card in my pocket began to pull me toward the abandoned building at the end of the plaza. The building was even more dilapidated than I remembered, but I knew what it was the moment I saw it: the ENCHANTED LIBRARY!

If there was one place where I would find answers, that was it!

Guard Plants

I reached the building, knocked on the door . . . and all the feathers flew behind my back to hide! What were they scared of?

I SMELLED TROUBLE!

"No one's answering," I said to myself after a moment. Then I gathered my courage. "Oh, come on, I need to get my snout on straight! I know how to **enter**! I found the emergency key the last time I was here." I turned to get the golden key that was hiding under the vase. But the vase was missing! Holey cheese balls!

I pulled the Golden Library Card out of my pocket and waved it in front of my snout. "Now what? How do I get in?"

At that moment, a group of mouselets walked up. One of them looked skeptically at me and then at the card. "Umm, sir, you do know that this great **palace** is abandoned, right?"

I turned red and stammered something like, "No! I mean, yes! Of course! Thank you for telling me. You're very kind."

As I spoke, I **backed up** slowly along the wall, until I disappeared from their sight around a corner of the building. The feathers were still attached to the back of my jacket.

"**What a fool I am!**" I said with a sigh. Then I peeked out from behind the corner and saw the mouselets walk away. "Who took the vase? And the key? And why?"

I gazed at the side of the building, stopping to look at the **ivy** growing along the wall. It seemed like it might be there to stop me from entering!

"Maybe if I move it a bit," I said, looking at the ivy near a French door on the first floor next to me. "There must be another entrance."

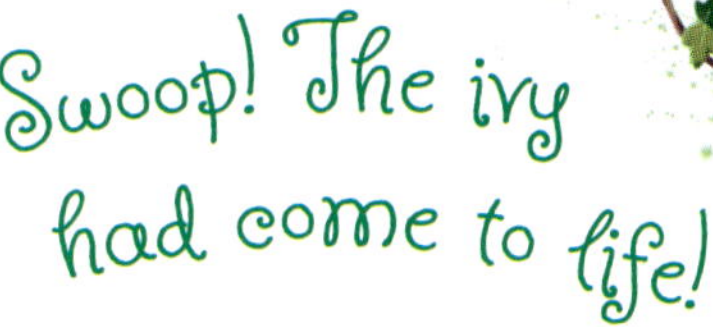

In an instant, I found that I had vines wrapped around my paws. Holey cheese! The plants were guarding the building! I whispered, "Excuse me, dear plants, I am a friend of the Enchanted Library and I have **permission** to enter! I can prove it. Golden Card, show yourself!"

The card began to sparkle its magic light at the plants, which squeezed me . . . in a **hug**!

Then the vines let go, gave a sort of bow, and disappeared through a crack in the door. Finally, they turned the handle from the inside and slowly opened it!

"Thank you so much, dear plants!" I exclaimed. With one pawstep, I was inside the Enchanted Library again!

After thanking the plants and sticking the card back in my pocket, I looked up to admire that magnificent library once more! But I quickly realized that something still wasn't right. The feathers had darted off to hide, as if they had sensed some kind of danger.

"It's the same library, but something's STRANGE," I muttered to myself, keeping my voice down, afraid that someone could hear me squeaking.

Someone like . . . Regulus!

"No," I said firmly. "That can't be. He was **turned to lead**! There must be some other reason his statue disappeared."

I sniffed the air. There was a slight scent of something burning, and it was unusually quiet.

Where were the Owlets?

Why weren't they dusting, and organizing, and singing?

What about Furry and Sophia?

Why couldn't I hear them bickering, like always?

I moved farther into the room, creeping cautiously on my paws. The Golden Library Card peeked out of my pocket, but stayed mostly hidden. I saw piles of books stacked here and there, and noticed a layer of **grayish smoke** that was accumulating just under the ceiling, clouding all the paintings of

Imaginaria,

the queen of Imagination, the Lady of Books and Creativity.

Oof! As I was looking up, I tripped on Furry's fantavacuum, which was abandoned in the corner. Strange! He would never leave it behind. He loved **fantavacuuming** fantastical creatures on the streets of New Mouse City!

"Imaginaria! Owlets! Furry! Sofia!" I called cautiously, still trying to keep my voice down.

But there was no answer. What could I do? I was moving through rooms one after the next, and it felt like walking through a maze of

SADNESS. I passed a finger across one of the columns and chills ran down my fur. A light layer of ash and dust covered everything.

What was happening?

Just then I smacked a paw to my forehead. "Of course! Imaginaria is a shape-shifter! She and the Enchanted Library are the same thing! Since I'm walking in the library, that means I can't see her in her human form. I'll probably only be able to talk to her through her image in the **Portrait Tower**!"

It took me a while to orient myself, but I finally found the right staircase and climbed and climbed and climbed, higher and higher. My paws were burning!

Once I arrived in the octagonal tower room, I ran to the wall that held Imaginaria's painting. But the giant **FRAME** held only a white canvas! Squeak!

"Now what?" I asked myself. "How will I ever be able to talk to Imaginaria?"

In my heart I hoped to hear her sweet and reassuring voice, but I heard nothing except total silence.

I didn't know what else to do. Then I felt the fluttering of feathers behind me. I spun around. "Oh, come on! Wouldn't it be easier for me to talk directly to an Owlet?"

One of the feathers darted at my face to keep me quiet. The feathers were much less cheerful now. They seemed frightened!

I continued squeaking under my breath. "Can you take me to Imaginaria?"

In response, the feathers all slipped behind the frame holding the white canvas.

Thundering cat tails, what was going on? Slowly, the frame opened like a door. The feathers had pushed it open!

I peered in and saw that the feathers had begun to float upward. A crystal staircase appeared one step at a time.

There was nothing left to do but follow them up the steps!

Heart pounding and fur trembling, I passed through the threshold of the magic portrait and began to

The Tower of Ideas

At the top of the staircase, an enormouse terrace materialized, towering over New Mouse City. I was at the top of **THE TOWER OF IDEAS**, the place where Imaginaria would write her beautiful stories in the air with her magical golden pen. Every day she wrote marvemouse ideas in the air. Then she spread them throughout the world!

This way, fantasy and imagination would never run out!

I looked all around. The terrace was full of piles of books and mounds of dried leaves, but something else was there, too.

She stood in the middle of the terrace, arms spread wide, her flowing hair and paper dress whirling in the wind.

What a fabumouse sight!

Furry and Sofia had spoken of it, but I had never seen such magic with my own eyes!

As I took a closer look, I could see that there was something strange happening. . .

I peered at the Queen of Imagination's face, but I didn't see her sweet smile. Her eyes were full of sadness — no, they were lifeless!

She rummaged through a book placed on a large lectern. A TEAR streamed down her beautiful face while her magic pen was . . . hitting the book?!

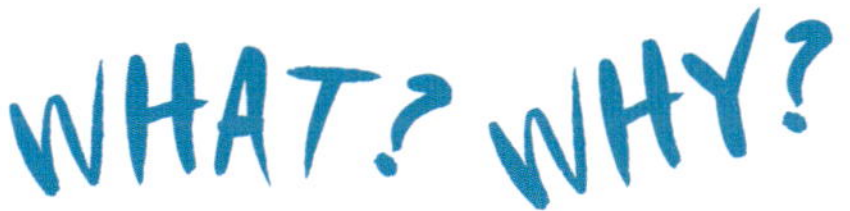

Instinctively, I dashed over to try to stop her, but I heard a strange hissing coming from the leaves that whirled all around. I froze — just in time!

A mysterious woman I had never seen before appeared next to Imaginaria. At just one glance, I felt myself overwhelmed with feline fright! I ducked behind an enormouse pile of books.

She was a beautiful but SCARY creature, with a horrible, scornful scowl.

The Golden Card hid deeper inside my pocket.

From the other side of the terrace I could hear a somber but familiar voice. "I think Imaginaria is moving too slowly."

Who had said that?

I couldn't see over all the books. Even though I couldn't tell who it was, I was sure that I had heard that voice before. It gave me chills!

The mysterious woman screeched, "Hurry up, Imaginaria! I'm sick of your dawdling!

What is she doing?

Get the precious words out of that book now, by the order of Witch Violet!"

I could hardly believe my ears. How dare she speak to Imaginaria, the Queen of Imagination, the Lady of Books and Creativity, like that?

To my surprise, my friend lowered her head and obeyed.

Using her magic pen, she pulled many floating words out of the book. They drew delicate golden loops in the air, and then — Bzzzt!

Witch Violet struck them one by one with an evil ray! The beautiful words transformed into treasure chests full of gold and silver coins, precious stones, and clothes **adorned** with pearls. Holey cheese!

The witch cackled. "Hee, hee, hee! I'm a genius! Using Imaginaria's fantastic powers, I can pull all the most precious treasures from books. I'm going to become richer and richer!"

Imaginaria lowered her wand.

The witch scowled. "Are those all the treasures in this book? I had hoped for more."

Violet shrugged, then held up a huge golden necklace covered with **emeralds** and fastened it around her neck. "How do I look, my beloved?"

My beloved? Who in the name of all things cheesy could she be talking to?

I still couldn't see this other person, but I would find out who it was soon enough!

Just then a huge cat wearing a wide-brimmed hat and boots popped out from behind her. I

"Extract the
precious words
at once!"

knew that feisty feline! It was **Mercutio**, one of Regulus's henchmen!

Squeak! Could he be Violet's beloved?

He jumped cheerfully onto the lectern and grabbed the book that had been stripped of its treasures. He put it under his arm and headed toward . . . Cheesy creampuffs, I couldn't get a good look with all those **BOOKS** piled everywhere! I darted past the next stack — and that's when I saw him.

Standing beside Leadness, the terrible fire-breathing dragon, was

Well, it was the statue of Regulus, anyway. The wizard was still lead, except for his face, which appeared to have chipped. It had regained its **grayish** color and usual sneer. That's who the terrible witch was talking to!

I was truly stunned. How could this have happened?

But I was even more shocked when I saw Mercutio throw a book at Leadness. The dragon used his flaming breath to incinerate it in an instant!

PHIUUUUUMMM!

My whiskers wobbled. How could they burn books?

I had to do something! I tried to dart out into the open, but the pesky feathers held me back. Then I spotted the crow **Korax**, another one of Regulus's henchmen. He quickly gathered up the ashes of the book. Then he put them into a bowl and began to mix them together, forming a strange brew as he sang.

"One pound of ash
of fantasy
plus thirty-three
eggs of an old harpy
and stain-free drool
for wizardry.
What will all this
come to be?
A wicked mask of
sheer beauty!
A mask that makes
the lead come off!
Caw, caw, caw and
scoff, scoff, scoff!"

Regulus cried, "Will you quit your singing and hurry up? It's bad enough these magic concoctions of **fantastic ash** take forever. Please don't make us listen to your squawking."

I watched as the crow and cat ran toward him. They began to rub the mixture on a part of his face that was still made of lead, while Mercutio said, "Have patience, boss. Try to relax and enjoy the process a little. We're starting with the fantasy ash mask, but we also had a scrub made of **crumpled fantasy pages**. Just wait until you see the results!"

Violet let out a little laugh. "Oh, a beauty scrub, too? You're getting so fancy, my dear Regulus! Ha, ha, ha!"

The wizard shot her a piercing look. "If it wasn't for these treatments, I wouldn't even be able to talk. At least they're helping me reverse the effects of the **leadifying spell**."

Regulus peered closely at Violet. "What are you

doing, my dear? Aside from making fun of me and wasting time with your treasures, that is?"

Violet's face turned a deep shade of purple. She looked like an **eggplant**! "Wasting time? Do you remember leaving me **IMPRISONED** inside a book for centuries before you could be bothered to pull me out, my fiancé? Now I need to make up for lost time! I need to recover all the **treasures** that have been stuck inside these useless books with no one to truly appreciate them! Now I will have them ALL! Understand? They must be mine. I will become the **richest** witch of all time! There will be no limit to my riches! You should be happy, since it will all belong to you as well."

As she continued to yell, I was lost in thought. Had she called him "my beloved" and then "my fiancé"? Those two were . . . engaged?

A gust of wind made a newspaper page fly up and hit me in the snout. I gave it a quick glance but then realized that it held the **answer** to my question. I read it quickly but carefully!

Squeak! So I had understood correctly!

THOSE TWO WERE ENGAGED!

6,543TH DAY OF THE THIRD FULL MOON

THE TERRIFYING EVIL ALLIANCE

BY OUR CORRESPONDENT LONG-TONGUE TOAD

The terrifying Regulus and the cruel Witch Violet have made a close and dangerous alliance. Well-informed sources tell us that the two most evil and frightening fantastical characters of the last few centuries have just announced their engagement.

There has been no official confirmation, but this could be due to the mere fact that no one knows who the relatives of these evil characters are. We don't even know their real names! Even if someone knew their families, it would be difficult to work up the courage to go and ask about them.

So instead, we ask ourselves: Are we about to witness the marriage of the century? Who will be invited to the ceremony? Who will have the courage to attend? How long will this couple last? Will the rest of the world survive their marriage?

TIMES

- - - - - - - - - - - - - OF THE SEASON WHEN

LATEST NEWS

Umm, I'm not sure I understood the exact date, but this page comes before my first fantastic adventure!

BY PRINCE GOSS IPPER

Witch Violet has disappeared! It seems that the witch was last seen shortly before midnight, walking the streets of a gnome's general medicine book. Witnesses, who prefer to remain anonymous for obvious reasons, say that she cried for someone to help her get out of the book, since her magic was not powerful enough on its own.

Could Regulus have had something to do with the disappearance of Witch Violet?

It seems that he has his eyes set on a new lady: Imaginaria!

Wondering what his plans are? That's easy! Destroy her so he can put an end to creativity and imagination!

Pull Out the Precious Words!

I was still shocked by my discovery, but **Violet's** shrill voice brought me back to reality.

"Here's another one of your books!" she yelled, letting an enormouse volume fall on the lectern.

"Pull out the precious words, come on!"

In my heart, I hoped that Imaginaria would rebel. I desperately wanted her to take a deep breath, lift her head, and take on the witch! But once again, my friend obeyed.

She lifted her wand in the air and struck the book — but this time, not a single word came out!

The wand straightened up, vibrated, and let out a few small sparks, but then it went limp.

Imaginaria lifted her head and looked at the witch with lifeless eyes. When she spoke, her voice was flat. "It's dead. We need to wait for it to recharge."

Violet stomped her foot. "No, no, no! This is the last thing we need! This pen is running out of juice more and more quickly!"

Regulus smiled, pleased. "I already warned you. You separated Imaginaria from the Enchanted Library and **weakened** her."

Korax nodded knowingly. "You tell her, boss!"

The wizard continued. "Now that you've taken her powers, you control her with your bewilderment spell. You can make her use the wand as you wish, but she can no longer feed it with imagination."

Korax squawked, "Right! Explain it to her, boss!"

"Plus, we are destroying all the books," Regulus went on, "so the fantastic energy is weaker and weaker."

"That's right!" the crow chimed in.

"Be quieeeeet!" the witch yelled, exasperated. Korax's feathers stood on end. "Quit explaining everything to me like I'm not capable of understanding! I know exactly what's happening here."

She took a deep breath. "We will wait. I might take a walk through the underground cellars, among the infinite rooms of treasures. Want to come with me, REGULUS, dear?"

My ears perked up. Maybe this was my chance to talk to Imaginaria!

"If you really want me to," Regulus said reluctantly. "There's not much happening here, anyway."

And so, as I had hoped, Korax and Mercutio lifted Regulus onto a gurney and followed Violet down the stairs. **Leadness** took off into the sky to stretch his long wings. I could finally come out of hiding!

I immediately ***DARTED*** toward Imaginaria, who was still standing in front of the lectern, looking out into nothingness.

I ran up and grabbed her hand.

"My friend! I'm here!"

She turned and looked at me.

Another tear streaked down her face, but her expression didn't change.

"It's me, the Fantastic Hero," I explained. "Don't you remember me?"

Imaginaria only sighed in response. The Golden Library Card leaped out of my pocket and flew into the air, spinning around her trying to get her attention. But Imaginaria didn't seem to care about the card, either. She gave us both a long, sad look — then turned her back and left! The Golden Library Card drifted slowly back into my pocket.

I was crushed. Was she ignoring me? Why had she **left**? Where was she going?

My brain was more scrambled than a plate of cheesy eggs. I didn't know what to do! It was obvious that Imaginaria didn't recognize me.

BUT WHY?

What had happened to her?

I was about to follow her when I heard a sigh coming from one of the stacks of books. I turned toward it and saw the leaves **shaking** and the books wobbling slightly.

What was under there? Oh, I didn't want to know! I'm too fond of my fur!

Before my eyes, the leaves lifted and revealed . . . the **Owlets**!

That's where the keepers of the Enchanted Library had ended up. They hadn't abandoned her; they'd been by Imaginaria's side all along — but they were **hiding** just like I had!

I hugged them. “My friends, thank you for sending me your feathers! Without you, I wouldn’t have known that Imaginaria was in trouble. But I really don’t know what to do now!”

A Simple Yballul

On the terrace I stood with all thirty-three Owlets, who had popped out from different stacks of books and leaves. Squeak, they were expert hiders!

"Friends, do you know where Furry and Sophia are?" I asked. "I'm sure that they would know what to do!"

The Owlets all began to talk over one another. "Whatwhatwhat?"

"Do you think that we aren't capable of helping?"

"Do you think the only thing we can do is dust?! How insulting!"

Oh no, I had offended them! What a cheddarhead! I quickly tried to fix my mistake. "No, not at all! The way you used your feathers was genius! But I don't know where to **begin**. I mean, what kind of Fantastic Hero am I?"

The Owlets flapped their wings, rustled their feathers, and dragged me into a

vortex of feathers and sparkles.

"Oh no, don't start with your whining!"

"A nice **VORTEX** should get rid of it, and you'll be good as new!"

"A rustle here, rustle there, we'll clear your head beyond compare!"

When they stopped, I was left spinning on my paws, **twirling** like a top, slower and slower and slower. Finally, I ended up sitting on the ground. My snout was still spinning!

"Umm, **th-thanks**, I do f-f-feel so much better!" I stammered.

"Good!" exclaimed **PHILOMENA**, the most selfless Owlet. "Now prepare a plan!

She looked me up and down, from the ends of my whiskers to the tip of my tail. "The library is an important place. It's the heart of fantastic energy and the place where all the infinite treasures are located. ***Every book held here holds priceless riches!***"

I felt crushed with responsibility. Holey cheese!

"I'm warning you, Hero, it must be a valiant plan!" PAULINA, the boldest, added.

"But wise!" Sheena, the most careful, specified.

"Yes, but most of all, it must be original!" clarified **Albertina**, the most creative.

"We need a plan — a good plan." I said.

Reena, the most distracted, exclaimed, "If I understand correctly, you need to free Imaginaria from the spell and get rid of the evil ones. Simple, right?"

How could she think that would be easy?

"Free Imaginaria from the spell? Right! Of course! But exactly what kind of spell are we talking about? Before, Regulus talked about a BEWILDERMENT SPELL! Could you give me some more information?"

Edina, the most intelligent, lit up. "Yes, yes, yes, I've heard of it. Great!"

My heart filled with hope. "Great? Do you mean that it's an easy spell to **reverse**?"

"Oh no!" she responded. "Great because I know of it. But I don't know how to reverse it!"

I deflated like a balloon.

The Owlet went on. "What I do know is that the spell deprives people of their free will. They must **OBEY** whatever order they're given by the person who performed the curse."

I nodded, thoughtful. "So Imaginaria can't do anything of her own free will, not even talk?"

Suddenly, I was filled with panic. "If Imaginaria can't tell us how to help her, there's no **hope**!"

The Owlets began to chastise me. "Quit your squeaking! You are the Fantastic Hero. You can, you must, and you will!"

Then Christina, the most studious, suggested, "If Imaginaria seems dazed and a little sleepy, you could try a simple ***yballul***!"

Tina, the most boring, added, "Good idea! And now, friends, we must find Imaginaria at once. We have to make sure she isn't causing any damage while she's DAZED!"

The Owlets all nodded and said in unison, "The Fantastic Hero can manage a simple yballul on his own, right?"

In the twitch of a whisker, the Owlets flew off.

The Wind of Inspiration

That's how I found myself alone once again, with a question on the tip of my tongue. "A *ybal* . . . what?!"

I felt more CONFUSED than Fantastic! I never imagined that I would say this, but I really missed Furry and Sophia!

I began to pace back and forth on the terrace, dodging the books and leaves. I squeaked continuously under my breath, "Yballul."

What could that word mean? What mysterious language were the Owlets speaking? And why couldn't they just wait a minute and explain it to me?

I clutched my coat and pulled it tighter around me. Brrr, the **WIND** was starting to pick up! I began to spin around aimlessly as the wind grew stronger and stronger.

I started walking again, and the wind began to gust even stronger than before! Moldy mozzarella, what was going on? A **STORM**?

Only then did I realize that the wind whirling around me was full of sparkly specks. It was the

Wind of Inspiration!

It was coming to help me! The hissing wind seemed to be telling me something. Was that possible?

Between one gust and the next I perked up my ears.

"Listen here, listen here! To all the wind gusts: Give the Fantastic Hero the intensive inspirational treatment.

He is a desperate case, we repeat, a desperate case."

"Squeak, I am not a desperate case!" I protested, "I'm doing my best!" But my voice got lost in the vortex around me.

I struggled to keep my eyes open as my whiskers fluttered and my tie smacked me in the snout. All this wind would knot my fur!

But then I spotted a bunch of golden letters that

twirled and twirled
and twirled

like socks in the wash!

The spin cycle suddenly stopped, and the letters bounced up against one another, forming the word:

ybballul.

But that still didn't make any sense! Luckily, the spinning started up again, and once more it stopped, with the letters coming together to form the word:

Crusty cat litter, that was it! "That's the answer! How did I not realize it before?"

Yballul was the word *lullaby* spelled backward!

Finally, I had figured it out: A yballul is a lullaby that doesn't make you **sleep** — it does the opposite. It wakes you up!

"Fabumouse!" I exclaimed. "Now I just need . . . to write one?! Um, where should I begin? I've never written a lullaby before, so I have no idea how to write a yballul!"

The Wind of Inspiration whirled up and around me again. I heard it hiss, **"All wind gusts! Turn around! This is a desperate, hopeless case! We repeat: hopeless! Activate the emergency maneuver! Everyone assume your positions! Begin the Storm of Inspiration Treatment at level ten!"**

That's when I saw a storm front advance threateningly toward me. Squeak! There was a flash of lightning, and a boom of thunder. All of a sudden, drops of freezing water began to fall. In the wind in front of me was a mix of

Images of Aunt Sweetfur reading me stories when I was **little** . . .

Grandfather William singing me a song with his guitar . . .

Thea and I scurrying about New Mouse City taking photos . . .

Me and Benjamin and Trappy waking up happy in a tent, ready for a new mountain adventure . . .

Scenes from my favorite movies . . .

LETTERS that spun and spun, becoming words and then sentences . . .

Eating one of Aunt Sweetfur's delicious meals . . .

Sentences that I had read in books that had been meaningful to me . . .

Words that had sparked strong feelings . . .

I guess you never know where the right inspiration will come from!

All of it mixed together, spinning and spinning. Slowly, the words lined up one after the next and became my *yballul*!

"I found the right words, I'm sure of it!" I yelled to the wind. "Thank you for your help. The next time I find myself short on ideas for one of my books, I know who to call!"

The **Wind of Inspiration** quickly transformed into a warm gust that surrounded me gently for one last good-bye, drying all the rain that had fallen on my fur.

"My friend, I'm always here for those who know how to open their hearts and minds."

I smiled, then smoothed my FUR and adjusted my tie. Winking at the Golden Card, I said, "Come on, friend, let's go free Imaginaria. It's time to break that bewilderment spell!"

Back and Forth in the Enchanted Library

I began to run as fast as my paws would take me down the long crystal staircase, until I found myself on the back side of the portrait. Then I stopped. I didn't know who or what I would find on the other side. I leaned up against the **FRAME** and pushed it slowly. A sharp light came in through the crack. I looked here and there, but the room seemed empty!

"The coast is clear!" I whispered to the Golden Card.

I pushed on the painting and found myself once more inside the ENCHANTED LIBRARY.

"Now where could Imaginaria have gone?" I asked myself out loud.

"Come this way, quickly!" whispered a voice behind me.

I jumped and spun on my paws, but there was no one there! I turned, and THERE WAS NO ONE THERE!

"This way!" the voice insisted.

As my eyes adjusted, I could see something in the wallpaper at the end of the room. An Owlet was pointing her winglet to show me the way! It was **Lina**, the shyest Owlet, camouflaging with the wall.

"Wow! Incredimouse!" I exclaimed. "You Owlets truly are masters of CAMOUFLAGE!"

She blushed and hooted, "Oh, thank you, it's my specialty. I don't really like being the center of attention . . ."

Then we began walking. Actually, I walked and she flew,

changing color based on the **wallpaper** we passed!

As we went down the stairs of Portrait Tower, I asked, "So, the Tower of Ideas is at the top of **Portrait Tower**? How is that possible?"

Lina cleared her throat. "Excuse me, Fantastic Hero, but I don't see anything strange about it.

I thought about it and smiled. She was right — it was fantastic!

We had passed through a few rooms, each one the same as the last. They were all empty, except for the piles of books haphazardly thrown on the floor.

I looked over at Lina. "You know where we're going, right?"

She gave me a look and shrugged. "Since

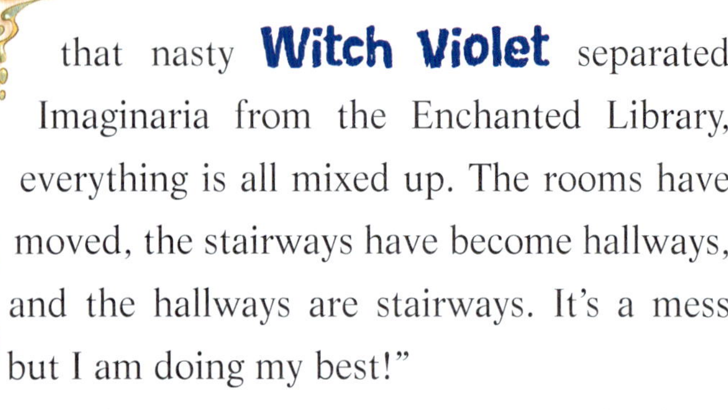

that nasty **Witch Violet** separated Imaginaria from the Enchanted Library, everything is all mixed up. The rooms have moved, the stairways have become hallways, and the hallways are stairways. It's a mess but I am doing my best!"

I sighed. "So, we're wandering aimlessly?"

She **hooted**, a bit offended. "Of course not! Sooner or later, we'll end up somewhere!"

We continued in silence, staying close to the walls of the rooms for safety.

In order, we passed through:

- The *Light Books Reading Room*, full of big marble tables and tall chairs with signs that said, YOU ARE ADVISED TO HANG YOUR BOOKS! WE ARE NOT RESPONSIBLE FOR ANY BOOKS TAKEN BY THE WIND.
- The *Reading Room of Voluminous*

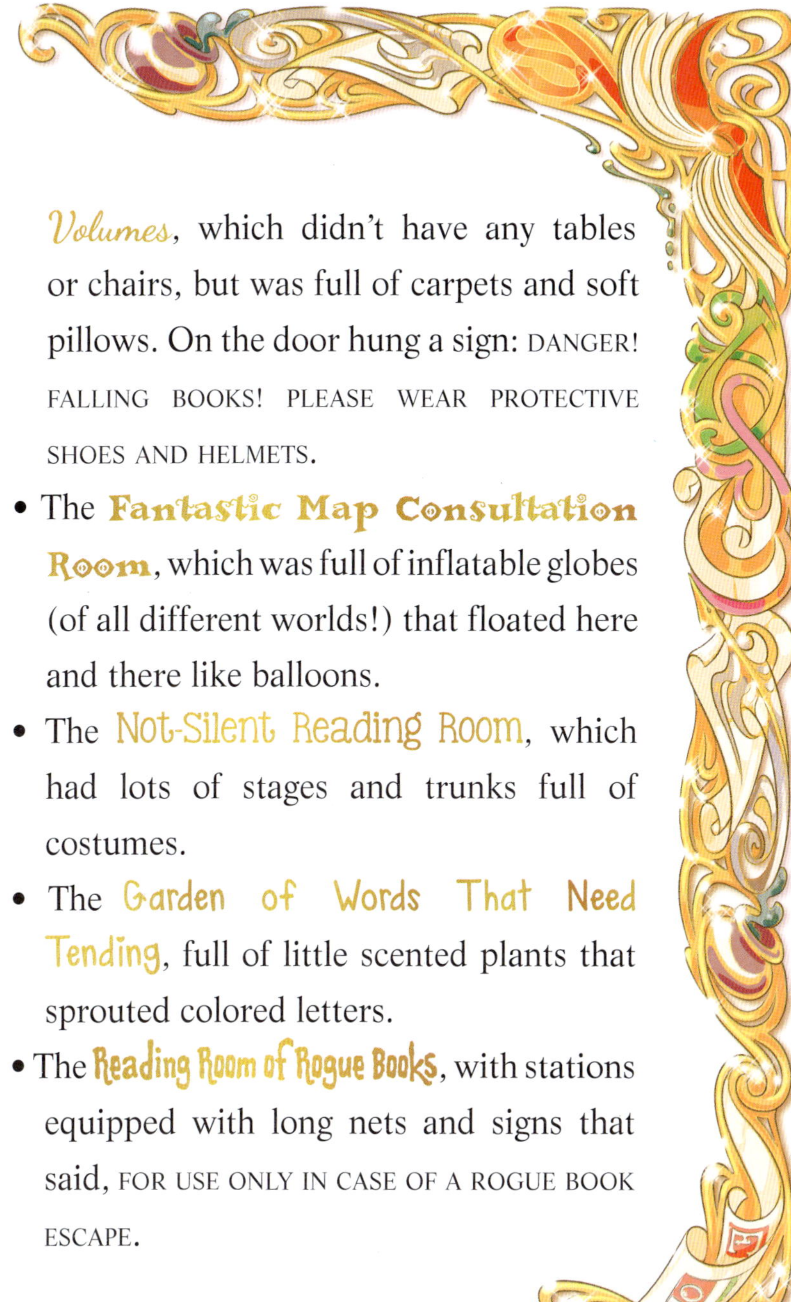

Volumes, which didn't have any tables or chairs, but was full of carpets and soft pillows. On the door hung a sign: DANGER! FALLING BOOKS! PLEASE WEAR PROTECTIVE SHOES AND HELMETS.

- The **Fantastic Map Consultation Room**, which was full of inflatable globes (of all different worlds!) that floated here and there like balloons.
- The **Not-Silent Reading Room**, which had lots of stages and trunks full of costumes.
- The **Garden of Words That Need Tending**, full of little scented plants that sprouted colored letters.
- The **Reading Room of Rogue Books**, with stations equipped with long nets and signs that said, FOR USE ONLY IN CASE OF A ROGUE BOOK ESCAPE.

Finally, we arrived in the Guest Bookroom, where I saw a marvemouse dispenser of tiny books filled with small tales and super-duper-short stories. Once we entered the room, we had to turn around because there was no other way out.

"Now what?" I asked. "Don't get me wrong, it's fabumouse to finally **visit** the whole Enchanted Library, but not like this! There's no one here, the books are thrown carelessly around, and I haven't found Imaginaria yet!"

After a minute, I realized that I was squeaking to myself. Cheese and crackers, where had Lina gone?

I looked around, worried. The Golden Card even leaped out of my pocket and flew through the Reading Room of Rogue Books to look for her.

The card peeked out the door that led to the **garden**, then immediately darted back and dove into my pocket, trembling in fright. What in the name of all things cheesy was going on?

I peeked out, quiet as a mouse, and saw what had scared the Golden Card. Regulus's dragon, **Leadness**, was flying overhead!

I ducked back inside so I wouldn't be spotted, but that's when I realized that **Mercutio** was walking along the other side of the garden, whistling. Squeak, now I was really in trouble!

Then I heard someone calling . . . from the wallpaper.

I looked to where the noise was coming from and saw Lina and the other Owlets!

"Hero, we need to get out of here without being seen!" Lina hooted.

I whispered back, "That's easy for you to say with your camouflage! How am I supposed to make sure I'm not seen?"

"Easy peasy," said Gina, the kindest Owlet. She tapped the wall with her wing three times, and a door that I couldn't see before swung open.

A secret passageway!

I scurried inside in the twitch of a whisker, just as Mercutio was coming closer.

"That was too close for my fur!" I exclaimed, walking down a **dark** and narrow passageway alongside my Owlet friends.

Katrina, the most curious, asked me, "Why didn't you go **directly** to Imaginaria's room instead of going all the way around?"

"Sorry, Hero," Lina said. "I got lost, but I was ashamed to admit it."

I sighed, then petted her feathers. "No worries, my friend. But don't ever be scared to tell me the truth!"

We turned another narrow corner and light flooded the hallway. The door in front of us was open, and it led to *Imaginaria's room*!

Imaginaria's Room

I found Imaginaria seated at her desk, which was a golden table inlaid with images of fantastic **characters** and legs shaped like a powerful lion's paws.

I closed the **DOOR** behind me, trying to figure out what she was doing. Was she reading?

But when I got up next to Imaginaria, I noticed that she wasn't doing anything at all.

She was dazed, staring straight ahead and pointing her magic pen at a blank page.

Crusty cat litter, it was awful seeing my friend this way!

I thought for a moment. "**HOW STRANGE!** Witch Violet left her with the magic pen?"

Xina, the most precise Owlet, wanted to explain. "The pen only answers to **Imaginaria**.

It won't work in anyone else's hands. So Violet doesn't mind if Imaginaria has it, because she knows that our lady is under her control."

I stepped closer and dried the **TEAR** running down my dear friend's face.

Then I puffed out my chest proudly and announced, "Don't worry, Lady of Books! I, *Geronimo Stilton*, the Fantastic Hero, have composed a ***yballul***! I will wake you!"

The Owlets stirred.

"Really? You wrote it?"

"Already?"

"Are you sure it will work?"

"You tested it out, right?"

"Don't cause any trouble, Hero!"

My enthusiasm vanished faster than a cheese platter at a rodent's birthday party. "Why are you all so worried? What danger could there be?"

They all ruffled their feathers.

"What do you mean what **DANGER**?"

"You're not going to treat our lady like a guinea pig, are you?"

"The wrong kind of yballul will put her into a deep sleep!"

"You risk her starting to . . ."

The Owlets all exchanged frightened glances. No one dared to finish the sentence.

I stammered, "Risk her starting to — to wh-what?!"

Trina, the most courageous Owlet, gathered her courage. "To snore!"

The Owlets all shivered at the thought!

My mouth hung open. What was the big deal with snoring? "It can't be any worse than my cousin Trap's snoring!"

My friends glowered at me, but they let me continue.

I took Imaginaria's hand, and she turned to me. She looked at me but clearly couldn't see me.

"I need to stay strong," I said to myself. "I need to put my all into this. It won't be easy to wake her from such a strong spell."

I cleared my throat, took a deep breath, and began to recite the *ybllul* that I had written earlier.

At first nothing happened, but I continued to sing the song to the end. We all held our breath and waited, but . . . nothing.

After a moment, Angelina (the most spirited Owlet) said,

"Well, at least she didn't start snoring!"

Her joke broke the tension in the room, and I knew that I couldn't give up. I repeated,

"NOW IT'S TIME TO SLEEP NO MORE,
NO OTHER SLUMBER, SNOOZE, OR SNORE.
LET'S ALL AWAKE AND GIVE A SMILE,
MOVING FORWARD, MILE AFTER MILE!
FEARS ARE GONE WITHOUT A TRACE—
TOGETHER THERE'S NOTHING WE CAN'T FACE!
DON'T BE SCARED, JUST TRUST US ALL.
LET'S TAKE HANDS, SO WE WON'T FALL!
SO MANY W_____ LEFT TO EXPLORE!
G____ TO PLAY, AND FUN GALORE!
S____ TO SING, AND MUSIC TO SCORE!
NOW IT'S TIME TO SLEEP NO MORE,
NO OTHER SLUMBER, SNOOZE, OR SNORE.
LET'S ALL AWAKE AND GIVE A SMILE,
MOVING FORWARD, MILE AFTER MILE!
THERE ARE B____ STILL LEFT TO READ!
A_V__T____ LEFT TO HAVE, INDEED!
LET'S ALL AWAKE AND GIVE A SMILE,
MOVING FORWARD, MILE AFTER MILE!"

GAME

On a separate piece of paper, help me complete the yballul!

SOLUTION:
worlds–games–songs–books–adventures

The third time I sang the yballul, something in Imaginaria's **eyes** changed. I kept going, and suddenly a light appeared out of nowhere and surrounded us like a sweet hug!

Finally, Imaginaria looked up and smiled at me!

The Three Treasures Spell

Imaginaria had returned! Squeak! I **hugged** her, my eyes filling with tears.

The Owlets were very jealous. They pushed and fluttered, so I had to move out of the way. They wanted Imaginaria all for themselves! For a few minutes, the room was filled with hoots of "Hug me, too!" and "We missed you!" and "Would you like some hot tea?" and "Look at me!" The Lady of Books laughed **happily**. She had a word, a hug, and a smile for each of them!

Then it was the Golden Library Card's turn. It flew **happily** all around Imaginaria.

Imaginaria watched the card dart through the air. "Dear friend, you are so **radiant**! I find you quite well."

Finally, it was my turn again.

*"My friend, my Fantastic Hero,
I knew you would come.
I never doubted that you
would rescue me."*

Mina and Xina felt the urgent need to comment. "Good thing you had no doubt! We weren't so sure!"

"Yeah, if it wasn't for us and our feathers, this mouse would still be wandering around in the dark!"

Imaginaria winked at me. "Of course I know you Owlets are indispensable! We couldn't get anything done without you."

The two Owlets puffed up their chests and ruffled their feathers delightedly. They were about to say something else when I interrupted. "Umm, excuse me? Remember that Violet and Regulus are still roaming free through the library!" I turned to Imaginaria. "I think we should give them a piece of our minds!"

She looked surprised at my enthusiasm. "You are in quite a courageous mood, Hero! Now tell me, what is your plan?"

I was squeakless. "Um? Me? Yes, well, I don't know. But now that you're awake, we just need one of your spells and —"

Imaginaria shook her head. "Oh no, you've misunderstood. This situation is very serious. Violet put a spell on me and forced me to extract treasures from the books, but before that, she stripped me almost completely of my **powers**. She only left me the ability to use my pen to do what she requested."

"So, what now?" I squeaked in a panic. "How can I save the Enchanted Library all by myself?"

Imaginaria smiled. "You aren't by yourself! Who said you were?"

I shrugged, disheartened. "Of course, excuse me, dear **Queen of Imagination**. I am here with you now. I know I'm not alone, but I don't have your magic power and I don't have a whisker of an idea of what to do."

"As usual!" huffed an Owlet.

Imaginaria seemed discouraged for a moment, but then she lifted her gaze. Her face lit up with a magical smile. "You know something, my hero? I am sure that with your resources you will manage! You are more worthy than you think! You should be more confident."

Cheesy cheddar, how could she be so sure?

One of the Owlets seemed to read my mind. "You might be more worthy than you think, but, let's be honest, what could you possibly do to **stop** Regulus and Violet?"

"Not to mention their evil henchmen Mercutio, Korax, and Leadness? They are unbeatable!"

"It's true! You seem more like a Useless Hero at the moment!" another Owlet remarked.

I looked at her angrily, but then I turned to Imaginaria and shrugged. I had to agree with them!

What could I do?

The Queen of Imagination said, as if it was the most obvious thing in the world, "There's just one way that you can help me, Hero. You have to go into the books and bring their true treasures back to me! When I have them in my hands, I will be able to regain my **fantastic powers**!"

My eyes widened in surprise. "Holey cheese balls! What? Travel inside the books? You mean that I need to go through all the books in the library? And skim them all from front to back? Every last one of them?"

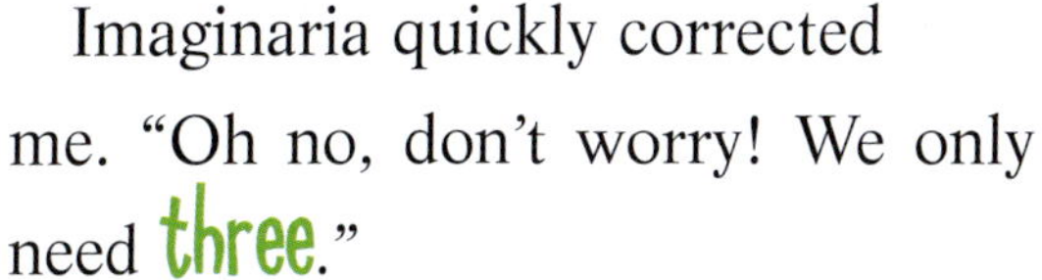

Imaginaria quickly corrected me. "Oh no, don't worry! We only need **three**."

Christina, the most studious Owlet, lit up. "The three treasures spell!

My snout was spinning. "What do you mean? What are the treasures that I need to get from the books? Jewels and gold, like Imaginaria got for Violet? How do I get into the books, and more importantly, how do you even enter a book?" I began twisting my tail into knots. "I'm not prepared for this! Can I just choose any subject I want?"

Imaginaria burst out laughing. "No, no, you are very prepared, my friend! You are the only one who can do it! With your fantastic pen, you can enter any book!"

"But how?" I squeaked. "I just take my *pen*

and —" As I reached to grab the pen out of my pocket, I realized something truly awful.

"Oh no!" I exclaimed. "The fantastic pen . . .

The Secret of the Fantastic Portrait

I looked at Imaginaria, feeling horribly guilty. "I meant to grab the fantastic pen, but then my cousin Trap arrived. You remember him, right? He tried to convince me to help with some new project and —"

Imaginaria tried to interrupt me, but I just blabbed and blabbed until . . .

"Well, well, would you look who we have here! The rat!" Mercutio meowed, poking his head through the doorway.

Squeak! They'd found us!

"Our boss will be happy to get his revenge on you!" added Korax, the crow.

The cat laughed, licking his whiskers. "Or he'll be happy to know that I stuffed myself. My mouth is already watering for roast mouse!"

"Don't you dare!" Korax squawked. "You know better than that! The rat belongs to the boss. He will decide what to do with him!"

The two of them began to **argue**.

Imaginaria took advantage of the moment. "Hero, down there!"

I looked to where she was pointing, toward a wall at the other side of the room. I could see a portrait of someone painted from behind.

That isn't very helpful. Why had Imaginaria pointed that out to me?

I looked at her, **confused**. "You need to go get the pen, Hero! Quick! You'll need it!"

I looked back at the painting again. What did it have to do with my pen?

It showed **someone** from behind, wearing a green shirt — no, a jacket — and he was looking out at . . .

I got a few steps closer and noticed that the figure with the green jacket was turned toward an office — MY office!

Squeak! That was my portrait!

I looked back at Imaginaria. "Is that the same fantastic portrait that's in my office?"

The Lady of Books whispered, "Of course! It's a **fantastic portrait** for a reason. It is a portal that joins our two worlds!"

I squeaked in embarrassment. "I didn't realize that!"

We stopped in front of the painting. "You really didn't know?" she asked. "So, all the times that you talked to the portrait, you weren't talking to me? I remember the time that you talked about how you'd made a tasty cheese fondue for dinner, and the time that you were sure you had made a good impression on your grandfather —"

I turned red from **embarrassment** and cut her off. "Umm, really? I don't remember that at all."

Holey cheese, why does everyone catch me talking to my portrait? This morning it was Trap, now it was Imaginaria.

"That's a shame," Imaginaria said, looking a little sad. "I thought you were confiding in me."

I glanced over at Korax and Mercutio, who were still arguing fiercely, and then looked carefully at the picture. That was my desk, but . . .

"I don't see the pen!" I exclaimed.

Imaginaria smiled, then put her hand on my back and gave me a gentle push. "Come on, Hero, get up close so you can see better!"

I closed my eyes, about to hit my snout against the painting.

But instead of hitting it, I felt my snout mush into what felt like cold, sticky gelatin!

I opened my eyes in surprise. My snout was inside my office!

Slimy Swiss cheese, I was the Geronimo Stilton in my portrait! And I was really looking into my office!

"Fantastic!" I exclaimed. Hopefully no one would wander in and find me hanging here.

Then I saw my pen, sparkling on top of the papers on my desk like a precious gem.

I stretched out my paw to grab it . . . but I couldn't reach.

I stretched farther and farther and farther, but it was still out of reach.

I would have to go through the painting completely, but just as I was about to do it, something behind me in the library grabbed my foot! **"Oh no!"**

I heard Imaginaria yell.

Mercutio and Korax had lassoed me!

Imaginaria went on. "I can't untie the rope, Hero — it must be enchanted!"

Squeak! This was the last thing I needed!

I felt a tugging, and my body began to pull backward. I grabbed the edges of the frame, trying to hold on, but Regulus's two henchmen pulled ***HARDER AND HARDER***. Holey cheese, I'm no musclemouse!

Suddenly, the Golden Card darted out of my pocket.

Imaginaria saw it and **shouted**, "Dear Card,

the portrait's portal only works for Geronimo! No one else can go through it alone. If you go, you won't be able to come back this way. You'll have to go all the way around."

"Go, Card, go!" I squeaked. "I promise I'll save Imaginaria and come back for you — rodent's honor!"

I heard the two henchmen laughing as they pulled, and my paws began to give way.

THEN EVERYTHING HAPPENED ALL AT ONCE!

The Golden Card darted toward the pen, aimed, and hit it like a golf ball toward the portrait hole!

The pen rolled closer and closer to me. I let go of the picture frame and grabbed it with my paw!

I cried, "Thanks, friend, I'll see you sooooon!"

I shot backward and popped out of the picture frame, pulled by the rope that Korax and Mercutio were holding. The two of them certainly hadn't expected me to let go so quickly. I hit them full on and sent them TUMBLING to the ground!

Squeak! What luck!

I had barely figured out what had happened when Imaginaria grabbed my arm and helped me to my paws. "Great job, Fantastic Hero! Brilliant idea!"

What BRILLIANT idea? I certainly hadn't done any of that on purpose!

Suddenly, Violet's yells echoed throughout the room. "What is going on here? Korax! Mercutio! Where are you?!"

The Owlets **hid** immediately. I turned to Imaginaria. "Quick, tell me what I have to do now that I have the pen!"

But she shook her head. "Not here. We need to get to **The Tower of Ideas**!"

I felt my fur turn white. "What? That's so far! I'm not sure we have enough time for that. Can't we just do it here?"

Imaginaria was determined. "Absolutely not. The **FIRST BOOK** you need is at the top of the tower. Owlets, buy us some time, please!"

Imaginaria grabbed my jacket and pulled me toward a hidden door in the wall, which was covered with decorative wallpaper. The last things I saw before I entered a tiny **passageway** were the diamond-speckled shoes of the witch and the wings of the Owlets, who were ruffling their feathers and hooting,

"Never underestimate the Owlets!"

The Flying Carpet License!

I found myself in a secret passageway yet again. How many of these passages were there in the Enchanted Library?

I followed Imaginaria along the tall and narrow hallway. There was always a dim light sparkling, which made me feel safe.

"Imaginaria, where is the light coming from?" I asked. "I don't see any windows."

She turned and smiled. "That's true, it's not coming from the outside."

I didn't understand! "But I don't see any lamps or lanterns, either."

She continued walking quickly. "You're right, this light doesn't come from lamps or lanterns!"

I threw up my paws. "So where is it coming from?"

"*You just have to use some imagination . . .*"

she responded, smiling, as if it was the most obvious thing in the world.

I sighed. "My dear friend, sometimes you're a bit too **mysterious**!"

She turned down a hallway that seemed a bit wider. Here, the pavement was covered by a long carpet covered in colorful squiggles.

"How fabumouse!" I exclaimed. "Why do you keep such a beautiful **carpet** hidden in a secret hallway?"

Imaginaria shrugged. "Because we need it to climb the tower, of course! Otherwise, how will we manage? It's the only way we won't be seen by **Violet**!"

"So, you made the carpet appear?" I asked in surprise. "I thought your powers weren't working."

She stopped and took me by the shoulders. Her eyes were full of **hope**. "Fantastic Hero, it's not me who made the carpet appear — it's you. Sometimes hope and imagination are all we need to move forward, and your heart is full of both! The important thing is to never give up, not even when things seem really difficult . . . or even impossible."

I stared back at her, SPEECHLESS. She was truly the Lady of Books, even now, even without

her powers and incredible magic.

"There is so much power in your words," I finally squeaked.

She nodded and took my paw. "There is power in all words. But come, we will dance a bit and soon we'll be at our destination!"

Huh? "Dance? What do you mean, 'we will dance'?"

She gestured toward the long carpet. As soon as I stepped a paw onto it, the carpet began to **wave**. Holey cheese, I had to hold my arms out to keep my balance!

"What's happening?" I cried. "I feel like I'm surfing!"

She nodded, amused. "Yes, that's the idea! **TIME TO TAKE OFF!**"

"What?" I yelled. Before I could say more, the carpet lifted up into the air and darted toward the ceiling! "We're going to splatter against the

wall like mouse omelets!" I cried in a panic.

Imaginaria laughed. "What wall?"

As I watched, the walls around us disappeared. Wow! We found ourselves **flying** through the pink sunset among the library towers. My mouth hung wide as I admired the streets of New Mouse City down below, where life seemed to be carrying on as usual.

A young mouse suddenly looked up. His eyes **lit up** at the sight of us, but then a friend called to him and he ran off, distracted.

Had he already forgotten about us?

Would he think about this moment later?

What dreams would he have?

Imaginaria's voice brought me back to reality. "Violet and Regulus are already up on the terrace. They must have sensed that we are on the move!"

I twisted my tail with worry. "Where exactly are we on the move to? And if Violet is here, do you think the Owlets are all right?"

She nodded firmly. "Of course. Don't underestimate them, Fantastic Hero! They managed to give us the time we needed to get here. Come now, it's time for us to land!"

I gathered my COURAGE. "Yes, okay!"

I noticed that Imaginaria was

looking at me expectantly. "What is it?"

"We need to **LAND**! Now!" she said.

I nodded. "Okay, so let's land."

She gave me a look. "Geronimo, you're the one driving this carpet! I already told you that I don't have my magical powers!"

"What?" I yelped, sitting down and putting my head in my paws. "You must be wrong! I absolutely do not know how to drive a flying carpet! I don't even have a **flying** carpet license!"

"Okay, let's pretend that it's a car," she said patiently. "Now park it carefully. You can do it!"

And **suddenly**, I found my paws holding a steering wheel. "Holey cheese balls!" I squeaked. "Where is the stick shift?!"

She laughed. "Dear Geronimo, I think that this carpet has an automatic transmission!"

I took a deep breath and tried to relax. I turned the wheel to the right, steering toward the terrace. "Um, how do I make it go down?"

"Try tilting the wheel down," she suggested. "And don't forget to brake!"

My fur turned white with fear. What had I gotten myself into? I lowered the wheel.

"**It's working!**" I squeaked happily. The carpet pointed toward the terrace at the top of the Tower of Ideas. "I feel invincible!"

But my confidence vanished in the twitch of a whisker. A moment later, I found myself snout-to-snout with Leadness, Regulus's **EVIL** dragon.

I heard the wizard yell, "Destroy him once and for all! Now!"

Squeak!

The Elastic Paper

"What now?" I yelled, trying to make Imaginaria hear me over the sound of the wind.

My friend looked Leadness right in the eye. How did she do that?

"Dear dragon, why do you let Regulus treat you like that?" she asked. "He always orders you around without even saying please!"

"You don't really think that the dragon will listen, do you?" I called in disbelief.

"Hmmmm," I heard Leadness moan, twirling through the air thoughtfully. "You're right — he never says please!"

I couldn't believe my ears!

Imaginaria went on. "I bet he never says **thank you**, either."

The dragon's giant eyes widened. "It's true! That's right! How did you know?"

She smiled. "The mean ones are all the same."

Leadness lowered his voice. "Do you know that he never says **hello** and never asks me how I'm doing?"

I was stunned. Was this really happening?

Imaginaria turned to me and winked. "Words are important, aren't they? *Thank you, please, hi, how are you —*

those really are magic words!"

She turned back to the **dragon**. "I'm so sorry that Regulus treats you this way. You should tell him how you feel."

"You're right!" the **dragon** cried.

"Right indeed," I chimed in. "But do you think you could do us a big favor? Please?"

Leadness looked at me through angry eyes. Eek!

Had I gone too far?

Just then Regulus thundered from below, "What are you doing, you dopey dragon? Loafing off? Don't make me repeat myself: Destroy him!

Leadness turned as red as the sauce on a double-cheese pizza. Uh-oh! He was about to breathe some serious fire!

"I beg you, dragon!" I squeaked. "Please spare us! Let us get down."

Leadness stared at me with flared nostrils. The heat around us grew and grew.

Then he hissed, "Okay, since you said *please*. From now on, I demand to be treated NICELY!"

"So, who is the fireball for?" I asked. "If you want to be treated with kindness, you need to treat others with kindness as well. I don't think that a fireball is very kind!"

But the dragon wasn't listening. He had turned toward the terrace, opened his jaws wide, and hollered, "Boss! Can't you say *please* every so often? What would it cost you?"

PHOOOOM!

A fireball headed toward the terrace where Regulus was standing, still half-leadified. The wizard's eyes widened in surprise. His dragon was fireballing . . . him!

Violet raised a **PROTECTIVE** barrier as I pushed the carpet's steering wheel farther down, trying to land.

Imaginaria cried, "Hero, as soon as we touch the ground, you need to enter the book that I point to! Take my *pen* with you so the witch can't force me to extract any more precious words. Maybe the books will be safe for a while!"

The wind blew against my snout. "Okay, put it in my pocket!"

Instead, she pulled out a small golden chain and put it around my neck. Imaginaria's wand had become a pendant!

"Thank you!" I cried. "I will protect it with my —"

But then a **VIOLET** ray thrown by the witch hit the carpet head-on, just as we were about to touch down. Imaginaria and I flew downward, each rolling to a different side of the carpet. We stood up at once, but Violet was storming toward us — and she looked furious!

"That's enough!"

she thundered. "Give me that pen at once!" She reached an arm toward me.

I felt the pendant move — squeak, she was

pulling it toward her with magic! Suddenly, Leadness landed on the terrace with a thud. "**Hey!** Leave him alone! He was kind to me, and —"

The witch didn't let him finish. She shot a ray toward him and — *bzzzt!* — made him disappear!

Squeak, she was merciless!

Regulus let out a cry.

"Nooooooo! My dragon! What did you do to him?"

"I sent him somewhere else," the witch said. "Calm down, you'll find him sooner or later."

Meanwhile, I tried to run to Imaginaria, but the witch cut me off with another ray. I noticed that Imaginaria was pointing to **something** nearby with her eyes.

I followed her gaze and saw an open book that was set apart from the others.

Trying not to move my mouth, I said, "*I have to go in there?*"

Imaginaria nodded, then darted toward the wicked witch.

"Imaginaria, what are you doing?" I squeaked.

She glanced at me. "I'm buying you time!"

"But for what?" I asked. "I mean, I don't know what to do! You need to give me some direction, draw me a picture, **something**!"

She stood tall before Violet and whispered to me, "The Owlets will help you!"

The witch was clearly surprised to see her standing there but burst out laughing. "Hee, hee, hee! It's really you! Tell me, what do you plan on doing without your **powers**?"

But I knew that Imaginaria had extraordinary resources that had nothing to do with magic . . .

"My dear **WITCH**," she said, pulling out a long

ribbon of clear paper from her magnificent dress. "Magic isn't everything, you know? I've learned to get by."

She showed Violet the **ribbon** of paper, which she held tightly at both ends. The witch laughed, lifting her wand to strike, but Imaginaria didn't flinch.

She cried,

"This is elastic paper, and I know how to use it!"

With a quick movement of the elastic paper, the queen managed to **FREEZE** the witch in place.

It was absolutely incredimouse! First, she wrapped the paper around the witch's wrist. Then, before **Violet** could do a thing, Imaginaria jumped up and did a triple somersault in the air, without ever letting go of the paper. She grabbed the witch's other wrist and made the paper whirl around at the speed of ***LIGHT***.

When Imaginaria's feet finally touched the ground again, both of Violet's arms were completely tied up in the paper! The Lady of Books's hair fell elegantly onto her shoulders and she turned toward me as if nothing extraordinary had just happened.

"It's now or never, Fantastic Hero," she said. "This paper won't hold for long! *Be quick!*"

Cheesy creampuffs, I still didn't know what I

needed to do! I tried to explain that to her, but meanwhile the **Owlets** had all lined up behind her in a warriorlike formation. They were ready for anything!

The Fantastic Spell

Violet's face turned the color of a ripe eggplant, while I was turning whiter than a ball of mozzarella!

The flock of Owlets divided in two. Some of them continued toward me, while the others went to support Imaginaria, who yelled, "***The fantastic pen!***"

I raised it reluctantly, but I really didn't know how to use it!

That's when the first Owlet landed on my paw. **Ouch!**

The second one flew under my armpit.

The third one hit me square in the back, and I

began to roll to the ground, doing a kind of crazy somersault. As I was spinning like a TOP, the fantastic pen lit up. A ray of light from the pen struck the book that Imaginaria had pointed out to me.

Then I understood: The Owlets had led me through a spell in their own way!

Fantastic spell*!

I didn't even have time to read the title of the book before the cover began to shake. Magic sparkles surrounded me, the pages fluttered, and then the book flew up and fell . . . right ON TOP OF ME! Squeak!

*The spell to travel inside fantastic books. It can only be carried out by the Fantastic Hero.

GAME
What book do you think I am going to end up in?
A A book about dinosaurs
B A book about pirates
C A cookbook

You will discover the answers on the following pages!

I closed my eyes, expecting the worst — but nothing happened! Or at least, that's what I thought. While my eyes were still shut tight, I began to hear the sound of crashing **WAVES** on rocks.

Then I felt the sea air and heard the song of a seagull.

I couldn't hear Violet **SHOUTING** at the Owlets anymore.

Squeak!

Where had I ended up?

A voice cut through my thoughts. "Fantastic Hero!

Finally! Can you hurry up? We don't want to get eaten by a shark!"

I recognized that voice — it was FURRY! I opened my eyes, and what I saw left me squeakless. I was on the plank of a pirate ship!

Above me the pirate flag waved. I saw Furry and Sophia standing before me!

Imaginaria's two helpers were tied up like hogs. A SCARY pirate was keeping them under watch. They even had a sword pointed at them!

I looked beneath the plank into the water and saw sharp shark teeth. Yikes!

"I've entered a book about PIRATES!" I squeaked in disbelief. "I did it! Hooray!"

Furry did not seem to appreciate my enthusiasm. "You've finally arrived, rat! I was about to get desperate! Your entrance was beautiful — a real scene stealer. But tell me, do you have a **PLAN** to get us out of here or not? I don't know if you noticed, but we are in the worst part of the story: the part where the pirates feed the prisoners to **SHARKS**! I knew you would come, so we tried to make friends with these nice characters, but now we're really pushing it."

Sophia sighed. "He didn't even have the decency to make his entrance on the deck of the **ship** like a true hero! Instead, he ended up here with us on this page, ready for the sharks!"

How fabumouse! Until now, I would never have thought that I could ever get inside a book!

The owl cleared her throat and turned toward the frightening **PIRATE** holding a sword. "It's just like we were saying! This is the Fantastic Hero, who has been sent here by Imaginaria to complete a supersensitive **MISSION**!"

I tried to sound authoritative and introduced myself. "Ahem, pleased to meet you, Mr. . . . umm . . . Sir Pirate! My name is Stilton —"

Furry threw himself to the ground, desperate. "Ugh, noooo, you managed to even mess up the basics! That's not how it's done, **CHEESEBRAIN**!"

What was wrong with what I said? As I tried to figure it out, all the pirates laughed.

When they finally calmed down, the pirate at the end of the plank said, "Ha, ha, ha! This fool is the one who is supposed to convince me that he works for the mythical Imaginaria?

I don't believe it!"

The Pirates of Infinite Abysses

A ship darts through the waters of the Infinite Abysses, while the black flag waves in the strong southern wind. The whole population of the Dry Waters recognizes them ~ and fears them. Panic strikes the piers when the lookout begins to yell, "The Lady Pirates of Infinite Abysses are here!"

At the helm is Lucy the Fearsome, the most dangerous pirate who ever existed. It is said that she can slice her enemies in two with her blade, that she can dance the tango blindfolded and on one leg, and that she can speak seventeen languages and seventy-five pirate dialects.

She counts on many other lady pirates who are always ready to fight at her side. They have never once thought about calling it quits.

Along with her crew, Lucy has discovered thirty-three treasures, explored five of the six Infinite Abysses, and defeated all the other pirate crews that infest these waters.

AYE AYE!

Hearing the voice, I realized I was wrong. The pirate was a lady. Holey cheese!

She turned to me, making a face. "Pleased to meet you, Mr. Fantastic Hero! I am **LUCY THE FEARSOME**, and I lead the Pirates of Infinite Abysses on breathtaking adventures." She sneered. "I should tell you that the scene on the plank ends on the next page. Very soon, you and your friends will be giving my regards to the **lovely** sharks swimming below you!"

Furry rolled his eyes. "Just as I suspected! The hero's entrance was totally useless!"

I tried to keep calm. "This whole story has taken me by **surprise**. What are you doing here? Imaginaria needed you in the library!"

Sophia squawked, "Do you think we don't know that? We came here to try to help her!

Books are our only hope!"

Furry added, "We landed on the wrong page. The pirates tied us up as soon as we stepped onto the ship, so we couldn't look for the treasure. Who knows where it is?"

"So you don't know where to look, either?" I asked. "Imaginaria only told me to find the treasures hidden in three books so that I can free her, but she didn't tell me where they were."

"Treasure? Are you talking about my treasure?" Lucy pressed. "Who wants my treasure?"

I clapped my paws. "So there is treasure here!"

The PIRATE huffed, "Of course there is! What do you take us for? We're pirates! It is clear in our job description — we always have hidden treasure."

I rejoiced. "Fantastic! Now tell me, is yours

the only treasure in this book?"

The pirates looked at one another and burst out laughing.

"AYE! You can be sure that, if there were others, we would find them!" Lucy gave a sly smile. "But ours is well hidden. None of the other characters in our story will ever manage to find it!"

Sophia crossed her wings and said, "This is our chance, Hero! Explain everything to her!" She lowered her voice. "I'm sure that these kind pirates will be willing to help us, once they understand what's happening."

With that, I began to tell the whole story.

When I finished, Lucy said, "All right, you two-bit hero! You say this Witch Violet is forcing Imaginaria to steal the treasures from books? And that you need ours before she gets her hands on it? Let's go get it together. But if you lied, if you aren't the hero that you say you are . . . we will soon find out! And there will be **trouble**! Aye!"

The other pirates yelled in unison:

"There will be trouble if you lie! Aye!"

Cheese and crackers, what kind of trouble?

I smiled at Furry and Sophia as the pirates untied them. As soon as her wings were free, the owl turned to Lucy with concern. "Ms. Pirate, you should know that you don't call him two-bit hero but Fantastic Hero."

"That's right!" Furry continued. "We are the only ones who can make fun of our rat friend!"

The pirate ignored them, then said to me coldly, "Control your friends, two-bit hero. I have very little patience for those who talk too much!"

The Treasure Map

As Lucy's ship sailed across the sea, the pirates moved confidently around the deck. I looked out at the HORIZON from the stern of the ship.

Furry walked up behind me. "Hey, rat, I can see that you're trying to act like a hero — but you're not very successful! It might be that green color on your fur . . ."

Squeak, he was onto me! "I'm very queasy! But shhh, I don't want anyone else to know."

Even though I was the Fantastic Hero, surrounded by terrifying pirates in the middle

of a fantasy book, I was still the same old Geronimo — with seasickness!

"Hey, two-bit hero!" Lucy called. "Here's the treasure map!"

I spotted her standing next to another pirate, who was holding a **scroll** in her hands. The rest of the crew gathered around.

I sighed deeply, trying to control my queasy stomach. Furry, Sophia, and I walked over.

"*Treasure Island* is thirty miles west," Lucy explained. "We'll get there by following the short route this way." She pointed to a route on the map.

I nodded. "Excellent! It doesn't seem far."

They all looked at me with wide eyes. "You clearly don't know how to read a **map**," Sophia said scornfully.

I wanted to spend as little time as possible on those roiling waves, so I cut the conversation short. "It looks like a fabumouse plan. We need to get to the **treasure** quick!"

Furry elbowed me but Jeanne, the pirate with the map, called out to the other pirates. "**AYE!** Prepare for the worst!"

The others all yelled, "Aye! For the worst!"

"Umm, for the worst? Why?" I asked nervously.

"Because of this!" Lucy said, passing me the map. She traced her finger along the route, pointing out:

- *The unpassable phantom rocks*
- *The cruel deafening mermaids*
- *The disgusting endless vortex*
- *The giant serpents' dark bay*

Slimy Swiss cheese, how terrifying! I tried to hide my fear. "Well, they're just names . . . right?"

The pirates looked SURPRISED. "You're really not scared?"

Sophia tapped me on the shoulder with her wing. "Didn't I tell you? This is the Fantastic Hero. He's not afraid of anything!"

The pirates looked at me with eyes full of admiration. Moldy mozzarella, what had I gotten myself into?

Meanwhile, Furry whispered to me, "I never would have taken you for someone so COURAGEOUS. But if you want to know my opinion, we're toast! Imaginaria will have to find new assistants after this."

I tried to look on the bright side. "But this is a map drawn by characters in a book. These places must be just LEGENDS, right? Everyone knows that monsters, mermaids, and endless vortexes don't exist."

Sophia looked up to the sky while Furry hollered, “It’s clear that you’ve never been inside a fantasy book! Of course monsters, mermaids, and endless vortexes exist here!”

I turned white. “Wait, what? We’re really going to meet all those MONSTERS?”

Lucy sighed. “Oh, for a moment I really did think you were Imaginaria’s hero. But now I see you’re just the same old fool!”

Another PIRATE shrugged. “Aye, it’s better that way! In every adventure, there’s a character who dies right away because he does something foolish. Now we have ours!”

The others all nodded, satisfied. “Aye!”

At that moment, Artemis, the pirate on watch, yelled,

“Storm’s cominggggg!”

This time, Lucy was the one to turn pale.

"Oh no! The unpassable phantom rocks are dangerous, but during a storm — there's really no way out!

"Pirates, take your places!" she commanded.

Pirates began running all over the deck. **Yikes**, Furry, Sophia, and I were just in the way! The pirates dodged us like traffic cones.

As the waves grew larger, the ship began tilting from side to side. Suddenly, I was pushed against one of the barrels tied to the railing. I found myself in a **cloud** of dust!

I began to sneeze. "Achoo! Aaaachooo!"

My eyes started to tear and I suddenly understood: That wasn't dust! I had banged into a barrel of . . .

"Pepper! My pepper!" Anne, the pirate in charge of food, yelled as she followed me with her sword. "Put your paws down! Don't touch your eyes!"

Luckily, Sophia grabbed me and brought me over by Furry, who was clutching the railing for dear life.

I heard Lucy's voice over the THUNDER. "The storm is pulling us toward the disgusting endless vortex!"

Jeanne hollered back. "Lucy, we need to get to the helm! We have to turn portside now, otherwise we'll end up inside the vortex!"

But Lucy was still far away, and there weren't any other pirates close enough to help.

At that moment, Sophia and I looked at each other and understood: The future of this ship and everyone on it depended on us.

We needed to take the HELM into our own paws!

I was about to jump into action when Lucy spotted us and yelled, "No! Don't do it!"

Jeanne begged us, "**Stay out of our way!**"

The magical moment had been ruined! Furry shrugged. "Okay, if they say so."

But this time I had a plan, and so I said, "Of course we will stay out of their way — because Sophia will **fly** us to the helm!"

The ferret burst out laughing. "With this wind? She'll never manage! She's just a brainiac!"

Sophia ruffled her feathers. "**How dare you!**" She took flight, grabbing me with one talon and Furry with the other. She fought the wind valiantly and flew us toward the helm!

"Squeaaak!" I yelled. "Great job, Sophia!"

All the pirates looked up in disbelief.

Furry cheered. "A moment of glory!"

"Pant! Puff!" Sophia huffed. "How much

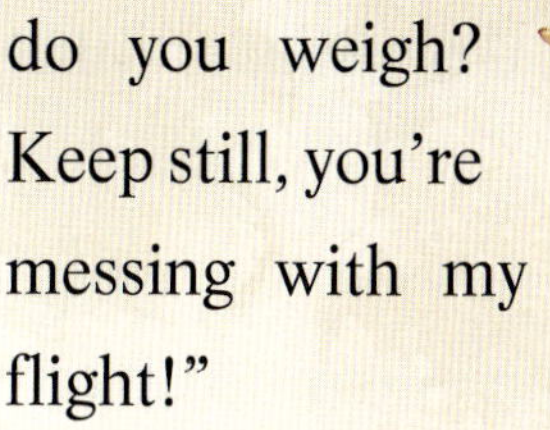

do you weigh? Keep still, you're messing with my flight!"

From below, Lucy yelled, "Incredible!"

As we flew over the helm I yelled, "Now, Sophia — let go!"

And Sophia let go! Yikes! I fell snoutfirst onto the helm, and Furry fell on top of me. I heard a BOOM, a BANG, and finally a really scary CRACK!

All the pirates turned white. Had we broken the helm?

But Furry and I stood up and . . .

"Ta-da!" I shouted, holding the chipped — but still functioning — wheel in my paws!

"Okay, now move it!" Lucy yelled. "Turn portside!"

Furry and both I put our paws on the wheel and turned it to the right. The ship turned, too!

A **ROAR** came from the deck below. "Noooooo!"

Furry and I exchanged confused glances. What? We were heroes! We were getting out of the storm and moving farther away from the endless vortex!

Lucy ran toward us. "What have you done?"

"We turned!" I pointed to our left. "We're leaving the vortex behind us. The sea is already calmer!"

Jeanne and the others surrounded us at once.

"You needed to turn portside!" one yelled.

Another added, "Portside — that means left! You turned us right! We need to go the other way!"

Sophia tried to **calm** them down. "The important thing is that we're out of danger! Now we can turn portside, can't we?"

But Jeanne shook her head, scared. "The vortex will block our path, and we will end up in an even worse place . . . the most **DANGEROUS**!"

All the pirates' faces were pale with fright — even more than mine!

Rats, this couldn't be good.

"Why is this spot more **DANGEROUS**?" I asked.

Lucy clenched her teeth. "This is where the **RELENTLESS KRAKEN** lives! You led us straight to his home!"

THE RELENTLESS KRAKEN

I repeated, "The Relentless Kraken?"

Sophia adjusted her glasses and began to rattle off information. "Precisely. It is a legendary SEA MONSTER longer than fifty Swamp Trolls lined up in a row, taller than three hundred polka-dot giraffes stacked on top of one another, heavier than 3,333 basilisks put together. The number of tentacles varies from eight to sixteen depending on the theory, but the main one suggests that . . ."

As Sophia spoke, I noticed everyone's eyes change. If they were scared before, now they were pawsitively TERRIFIED.

Something told me that it wasn't just what

Sophia was saying that made them look that way.

Nervously, I asked, "He's behind us, isn't he?"

Sophia and I turned quickly. A large **tentacle** as big as an oak tree emerged from the water!

Furry screamed,

"THE KRAKEN!"

In a flash, a dozen tentacles poked out of the sea and wrapped around the ship. "Save yourselves!" we **yelled**, running in all different directions.

Lucy climbed to the top of the main

mast. "Pirates! Companions of a thousand adventures!"

They all stopped and looked up. She stood **BRAVELY** amid the thrashing tentacles. "We have seen a lot, and together we will see much more. If we are **united**, we can get through this just like we always do! Remember: Keep calm and work as a team. Hands on your swords; we are the Pirates of Infinite Abysses! Aye!"

All the pirates responded as one. "Aye! We are the Pirates of Infinite Abysses! Long live adventure!"

Squeak, their loyalty made my **heart** swell!

It seemed like everyone had regained their courage. They could rely on one another!

Jeanne lifted her sword in the air and yelled, "Hooray for Lucy the Fearless!"

I followed her, yelling at the top of my lungs.

"Hooray for Lucy! As long as we have her, nothing can defeat us!"

I had no sooner squeaked those words than — **SQUISH!** An enormouse tentacle crashed into Lucy, wrapped her in its coils, and delivered her right into the kraken's mouth! Nooooo!

For a moment, everyone stared at the place she had just been. In that unreal silence, Furry muttered, "I think you bring bad luck, rat!"

Jeanne cried, "I don't believe it! Lucy!"

I began to think as fast as I could. The other tentacles had grabbed many of the other pirates already, and I saw one that was about to snag me, too! As fear **MELTED** my paws like Brie in the sun, I remembered that Imaginaria needed me.

Everyone was depending on me. So, I needed to do something!

I suddenly had an idea! An idea that made my heart leap, which spurred on my paws — and I began to run!

I threw myself toward the barrels, yelling, "Hey, you big SQUID, come and get me!"

Anne the cook yelled, "Careful, that's my —"

I didn't stop to listen to her — I just kept running. Everything happened in the twitch of a whisker:

I grabbed on to the barrel.

The tentacle grabbed me and the barrel, then moved us toward its mouth!

The Relentless Kraken wanted to eat me in one gulp . . . and that's exactly what I had hoped! That was my plan. Maybe it was a bit bold, but what choice did I have? After all, wasn't I the Fantastic Hero?

The tentacle squeezed and squeezed, until the barrel broke!

I heard Sophia yell, "Oh no! Fantastic Hero, you can't go out this way!"

The tentacle released me into the kraken's enormouse mouth . . . and I was surrounded by darkness.

It was a humid **darkness** with a terrible stench! Yuck!

All I could think was *What in the world was I thinking? Why do I have to be a hero?* But I could never have abandoned the pirates without giving my all. Then tears welled up in my eyes and . . .

"ACHOOOO!" I sneezed.

It was the pepper — the pepper that was in the barrel that the kraken was pouring down his throat!

"Maybe it's working!" I muttered. "I love when outrageous plans actually work!"

Suddenly, everything began to jump. I found

myself bouncing up and down. Then I was struck with a super-strong wind and —

"AAAAAAAAGHOOOOOOO!"

Lucy, the other swallowed pirates, and I were all spat out of the kraken during an EPIC sneezing fit!

We ended up back on the ship's deck along with the rest of the **fish**, various bits of wreckage, and a strange yellowish sludge that I believe was . . .

"**SNOT!**" Sophia exclaimed, examining it disgustedly. "Some scholars believe that it makes a great superglue!"

The monster fled, sneezing furiously.

I tried to clean myself off, disgusted, but suddenly I found myself in the air! The pirates were lifting me up in triumph.

"You saved Lucy! You beat the Relentless Kraken!"

"What courage! What genius! What a hero!"

I blushed. "Oh no, it was just luck. Now can you put me down?"

Lucy's voice cut through the noise. "Let him breathe!" Then she gave me a slight bow.

"I was wrong about you, **FANTASTIC HERO**. I owe you my life. How can I repay you?"

I shook my snout. "Just help me get the treasure to save Imaginaria!"

Lucy nodded seriously. "Of course, anything for Imaginaria. Jeanne, map out a new course!"

Jeanne responded, "No need, I've already done it. If my calculations are correct, we should be able to see the island now!"

We dashed to the bow to gaze out on the horizon. But what we saw left us breathless. There was no island. There wasn't even any sea. There was no water, no sky . . . NOTHING.

There was just endless **BLANKNESS**. Endless white paper.

Sophia muttered, "The white nothingness!"

Furry tugged on his fur. "No! Not the white nothingness!"

"*The white nothingness?*" I asked. "What

is that? What does it mean?"

Lucy was the one to respond. "It means that it's too late, Hero. The witch you spoke of has already taken our **treasure**."

Sophia added, "She erased the pages of the book. All that's left is a blank white page . . ."

THE WHITE NOTHINGNESS

While I was busy inside the pirate book, back in the Enchanted Library, Violet was about to burst into a fit of rage.

Imaginaria spoke quickly. "**Owlets**, hide yourselves! The hero is in the book, and I can manage here on my own!"

The Owlets nodded, and in the flap of a wing, they disappeared.

The witch, meanwhile, shredded the **elastic paper** around her arms into pieces with her shrill shouts. "How dare that rat take my wand? Who does he think he is?!"

Imaginaria corrected her. "You mean to say *my* **wand**! That pen is *my* magic wand."

The witch approached her, hissing. "You don't possess anything anymore! I separated you from your library. I forced you to empty and destroy your precious books. You are powerless! You are weak! You trust in a hero who is nothing more than a fool! You belong to me. Other than a few scraps of paper, what else do you have left?"

Imaginaria smiled a smile that lit up everything around her. "Oh, that's easy: I'm left with hope!"

The witch looked up to the sky. "Hope? You were right, Regulus, she's terribly naive!"

Imaginaria pretended to be surprised. "Naive? Maybe, my dear witch. But let me tell you, I think you need a bit more imagination!"

"Boring!" A voice came from behind them.

It was REGULUS, his face a grimace. "So much chatter! Who cares about hope, or the wand, or imagination?"

Violet crossed her arms, offended. "Without the *pen*, Imaginaria can't pull any treasures out of the books for me! I don't have enough yet — I need **MORE**!"

Regulus sneered. "My dear and cruelly marvelous beloved, don't you think it's more important to [illegible] the books so that I can be free?"

The witch torched him with her gaze. "Absolutely not! Before burning them, we need

to extract their treasures! You promised! It's the least you can do, since you left me imprisoned for so long!"

Regulus's eyes were icy. "If it's so important to you, why don't you go into the book and pull out the wand yourself?"

"I . . . well . . ." she stammered, taken by surprise.

The wizard took advantage of her uncertainty. "Oh, don't tell me you're scared! I know that you were stuck inside a book, but how bad could it have been? It's not as though you were frozen in place like I am! Of course, it's thanks to me that you're finally free. If my henchmen hadn't freed you —"

"It took you centuries to pull me out!" Violet shrieked. "I should leave you leadified for eternity!"

He ignored her. "Don't be so scared. You don't know that you'll end up in another trap if you go into a book. If you want the treasure that badly, then go, go . . . at your own risk!"

But Violet wasn't listening anymore. Instead, her face lit up. "I will send someone else to go get the **wand** and teach that old rat a lesson!"

Then she raised her wand, pointed it toward the pirate book, and muttered:

"From the whitest nothingness
an army appears, and makes a mess!
Here's your order, Paper Eater:
Find the hero before he can meet her!
Bring the magic wand to me,
your most dearly beloved lady!
And if this is something you can't complete,
I'll turn you into a golden love seat!"

A purple ray shone at the book as the witch cackled in triumph. She didn't realize that Imaginaria was muttering some words of her own, which the purple ray carried along with it:

"Small little creatures involved in this caper,
listen to this lady dressed all in paper.
I have no powers and no gold anymore,
but all my creatures, even you, I adore!
I know who you are, and I know what you do.
Now hear me tell you something true:
When you need to rest for a while,
ask the hero — he'll help with a smile!"

What Is a Pirate Without Her Treasure?

On the deck of the pirate ship, Lucy was devastated. "The island, the treasure, IT'S ALL GONE. There's nothing left!"

I tried to console her. "Don't say that. You have your ship, your crew . . ."

She interrupted me. "We don't have a mission now! What is a pirate without her treasure?"

I was about to respond when Furry yelled, "Look there!"

We all turned to where he was pointing. In the white nothingness, some DOTS had appeared. They seemed to be getting bigger and bigger!

We began to hear a kind of buzzing that was getting louder and louder.

zzZZzZ!

zzZZzZ!

zzZZzZZ!

I squinted to try to get a better look. They were . . . they were . . .

"**Woodworms!**" Sophia yelled in alarm, her feathers ruffled.

The name sent everyone into a frenzy!

Everyone seemed to know what they were — everyone but me!

I turned to Sophia and Furry. "Um, woodworms? Okay, I can handle that, I think."

The ferret grabbed my snout with his paw and turned me toward the woodworms, who were now visible on the horizon.

That's when I got a good look at them.

They were enormouse and **ARMORED** like

THE PAPER-EATER WOODWORM is a fantastic character that can be quite annoying: They are so insatiable that they often don't even look at where they put their sharp teeth. They move in a swarm of hundreds of insects and are a glutton for black and blue ink. They often suffer from bellyaches followed by insomnia.

a bunch of soldiers! They were **FANGED** with sharp teeth that gnashed up and down!

I yelled, "Why, oh why, oh why does everything happen to me?"

I was ready to give up when Lucy lifted her sword and yelled, "Pirates of Infinite Abysses, **FANTASTIC HERO**, we must stop the invaders! Aye!"

Everyone yelled, "**AYE!**"

Then they all turned to look at me.

Trembling, I raised my fantastic pen. I wanted to yell out "Aye!" also, but because of my fear a strange, strangled sound came out.

"Yeee!"

The woodworms darted toward the first ring of pirates, who were all ready to **fight**! But the woodworms **buzzed** around, zigzagging their way up and down the bridge, the masts, and the sails.

"What are they doing?" I asked Lucy. "Are they scared of fighting you?"

The pirate responded, "I think they're **LOOKING** for something. But what?"

I shrugged. "No idea!"

At that point, Sophia hit me on the head and Furry jumped on my paws. Oof! Together they yelled, "What do you mean, you have no idea? **Wake up!** The paper-eater woodworms are working for Violet, you cheesebrain! They are looking for you! Or rather, they're looking for Imaginaria's **wand**!"

I turned white. "I hadn't thought of that!"

Just then, a swarm of woodworms spotted me. They were heading right for me!

"Squeak!" I shouted, running as fast as my paws would take me.

"We will defend

"EVERY MOUSE FOR THEMSELVES!"

you, Hero!" Lucy cried. "Whatever it takes!"

With that, she stepped between me and the nasty insects and began a battle of **SWORD** versus teeth!

"Pirates, cover the hero and his friends!" Lucy commanded.

The pirates formed a circle around us, fighting bravely.

Sophia's wings drooped. "We'll never make it. We'll be **eaten**. We haven't even found one treasure, and Imaginaria needs three!"

"That's true, there's no more treasure here," I said thoughtfully. "So we need to go to another **BOOK** and look for another treasure!"

Sophia stared at me, stunned, "I didn't think you were that cruel. You want to abandon the pirates to the woodworms?"

I shook my snout. "Of course not! The woodworms want me. If I go, they will follow and leave the crew alone!"

Lucy overheard me. "No, hero, we will **defeat** them! Then you will be safe and can go look for other treasures!"

Her face fell. "After all, we have nothing left to lose."

I walked over to Lucy and stood behind her as she slashed at the woodworms. "My friend, I've wanted to tell you this for a while," I began.

She turned slightly, without pausing in her fight. "Tell me, Hero — I'm listening!"

"You say that you lost your reason for being, but that's not true," I said. "A chest of gold doesn't make a pirate. Boldness, courage, dangers to face, and breathtaking adventures to live through on the **seas** do!"

Lucy's face lit up as I waved the fantastic pen. I was getting ready to do the **somersault** the Owlets had taught me, so that I could leave this book and dive into another one!

The woodworms stormed me as I yelled, "Furry, Sophia, somersault! Follow me!"

GAME
What book do you think we will enter next?
A A book about plants
B A book about art history
C A joke book

I did a very messy somersault, holding the pen up high.

"Thanks, Pirates of Infinite Abysses!" I squeaked. "Even if we didn't find the treasure, we had a fabumouse adventure together!"

I felt a spark light in my heart. I hadn't found

It truly was a breathtaking adventure with loyal friends!

one of Imaginaria's treasures. But there was something here that was better than any treasure a mouse could imagine!

The horizon-page was turning to take us to another book. I could see the woodworms slam into it, stunned. They couldn't pass through!

Lucy's voice echoed behind me. "You're right, Fantastic Hero! Many more adventures await us. Thank you! And be **careful**!"

Then the horizon closed, the page turned, and

You will discover the answers on the following pages!

Furry, Sophia, and I found ourselves in a new book.

I looked around: There was nothing but trees as far as my eyes could **see**. "What book did we end up in this time?"

Sophia composed herself and explained, "We're in the book on the terrace that is physically closest to the one about pirates."

"How do you know that?" I asked.

She lifted one eyebrow, like she always did when I asked obvious questions. "Because you aren't capable of opening **PAGES** that are farther away."

Furry stretched his paws and rolled his eyes. "You really are a cheesebrain, for a Fantastic Hero!"

Queen Roseberry

Meanwhile, in the Tower of Ideas, Violet and Regulus were whispering to each other. Imaginaria strained to hear what they were saying. A paper-eater woodworm had returned to the terrace empty-handed, but with information: The Fantastic Hero had left the pirate book!

"To go where?" the witch yelled, furious.

The woodworm didn't know!

"But I do," murmured the Lady of Books to herself. "Geronimo ended up in the next book!"

Swiftly and gracefully, she used her feet to scatter the nearby books to confuse the witch.

Regulus noticed and laughed. "Look, she just moved all those **BOOKS**. I think she knows where to find the rat!"

Imaginaria shrugged her shoulders. "I don't know what you're talking about."

Violet began furiously leafing through nearby books. Suddenly, a satisfied **snarl** appeared on her face.

She opened one book and triumphantly showed it to Imaginaria. "Here he is. I found him! In a book whose treasures I already took! That rat doesn't have the faintest idea what a real **treasure** is."

The Lady of Books looked at the pages and saw the illustration of a rodent (me!) bowing before a super-tall queen with skin as green as the leaves of the oak trees that stood all around. "**THE BOOK OF EVERGREENS**," she muttered. "Good."

But Violet burst out laughing. "Good, you say? My woodworms won't let me down this time, otherwise I'll turn them into **golden** furniture! You, remind the others!" she added, pointing at

the woodworm who had brought her bad news. The insect buzzed away in a flash, scared, but not without a glance back at Imaginaria's reassuring smile.

Out of the corner of her eye, Imaginaria peeked at the pages of the book on the ground, where I was talking to the Queen of the Evergreens . . .

"It's an honor to meet you, Your Majesty!" I said. "I am the Fantastic Hero, and this is Furry and Sophia, Imaginaria's fantastic helpers. We are on a mission to save the Lady of Books!"

But the QUEEN, who was spinning a delicate crystal crown shaped like upside-down tulips on her head, seemed distracted. She seemed to be worried, but why?

I hadn't even told her about the terrible DANGER yet!

Maybe Violet had already struck here? Or maybe the queen was so tall that my voice hadn't reached her?

"I'll handle this," Sophia cut in, shaking her wings and flying up near the queen's face.

"Your Royal Magnificence," she said snobbishly, "allow me to speak for my companion, who may have irritated you with his squeaking."

The QUEEN snapped out of it and bent down to get a closer look at us. "Oh, no, no, no, excuse me, small fantastic creatures! Where were we? As I was saying, I am Roseberry, the Queen of the Evergreens. My people greet you with respect and with friendship."

Furry looked around and scratched his head. "Um, thank you, but . . . where are your people,

exactly? What queen goes around all by herself? There isn't a guard, or the chattering of a handmaiden, or a valet. Who is **protecting** you?"

This time, I was the one who elbowed him. "Come on, Furry, do these seem like appropriate questions to ask?"

But Roseberry sighed. "Oh, don't worry, **FANTASTIC HERO**. Your friend is right. My people do not love me very much, I'm afraid.

I have taken shelter here in my beloved **forest**."

Her voice got soft, and she looked sad. "You know, I don't think that I'm such a great queen. I've only been queen for two days, and no one takes me very seriously. I am a bit **shy**. My walk isn't confident enough — the leaves don't shake when I walk! — and everyone says I don't have enough strength to **rule** or defend our kingdom!"

I was shocked. "But, Your Majesty, those aren't the traits that make a good **LEADER**! You need other important qualities —"

"**NO, NO, NO!**" cried

a voice from behind us. I turned around and saw other evergreens. They poked out from behind the trees. They all had green skin, and when they walked, the leaves trembled.

The one who had spoken looked at the queen with disdain and then turned toward us. "If you need help, strangers, you'd better ask me. I am Sir Vineous, and the queen will surrender her scepter to me."

Roseberry and Vineous

Roseberry was the second child of King Strong Branch and was raised happy and free in the forest.

She was a reserved child of very few words. Her father said she was too shy to be a princess. But in the end, that wasn't that **IMPORTANT**. She wasn't first in line for the throne, anyway!

The future of the Kingdom was safe in the hands of the throne's successor, her brother, Sprout. He stood as tall as a giant sequoia, towering over everyone. He was always accompanied by their cousin Vineous, who was a few years younger. The two cousins were inseparable! Together, they had explored every corner of the **world**, even bringing back new seeds for the precious plant sanctuary.

One day, Roseberry wanted to go with them. In the beginning, they wouldn't let her because it was too dangerous.

The Book of Evergreens

There had been raids by **EVIL** wizards, and they didn't want to risk it. But then Sprout thought that it would be nice to encourage Roseberry and help her find confidence in herself. So, the three left together on an adventure.

But Roseberry soon got lost, and the two others had to go down an unknown path to **look** for her. That is where they found her – but they also found an evil wizard!

Sprout was so fascinated by the wizard's power – a **power** much greater than any he would have as King of the Evergreens – that he decided to follow him.

It wasn't Roseberry's fault that the evergreen people were abandoned by their future King. She couldn't help that Sprout had a thirst for power! But Vineous never forgave his cousin for getting lost.

Vineous frowned. "After what happened, surrendering to me is the least you could do. I knew that crowning Roseberry queen would lead to **disaster**."

I was terribly confused! Not even Sophia seemed to understand what was happening, which made me feel better. "What exactly happened that was so terrible?" she asked.

The queen's eyes watered. "The **unthinkable** happened. Our treasure disappeared! In a flash! And in its place, all that's left is —"

"The WHITE NOTHINGNESS!" I exclaimed.

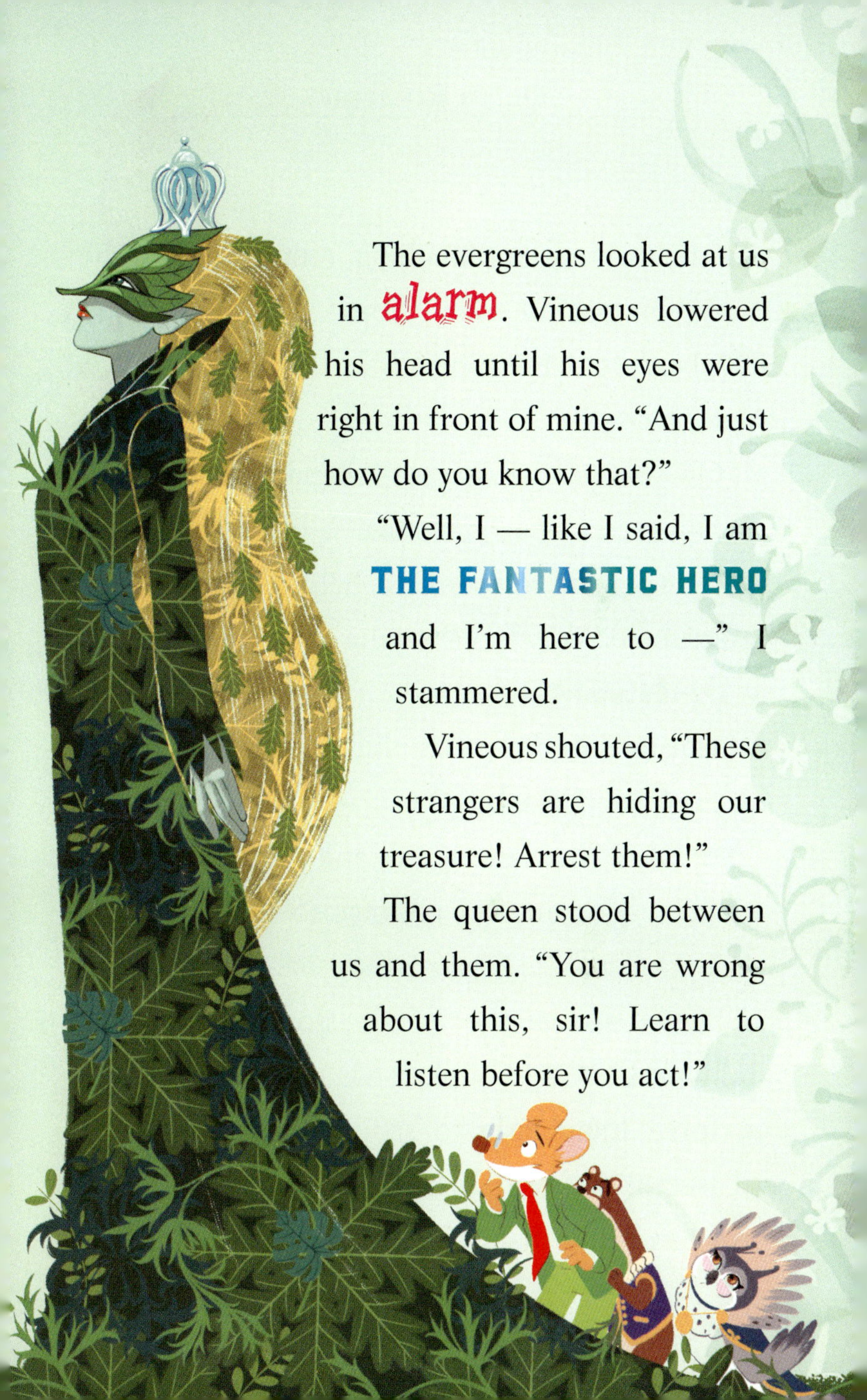

The evergreens looked at us in **alarm**. Vineous lowered his head until his eyes were right in front of mine. "And just how do you know that?"

"Well, I — like I said, I am **THE FANTASTIC HERO** and I'm here to —" I stammered.

Vineous shouted, "These strangers are hiding our treasure! Arrest them!"

The queen stood between us and them. "You are wrong about this, sir! Learn to listen before you act!"

Vineous burst out laughing, then turned to the evergreen behind him. "You see it, too, right? Roseberry can't govern. She is too naive, too weak, too —"

"Oh no," said Roseberry, hands on her hips. "I can accept that you have it out for me, but these strangers are here to help us. Before you interrupted, they were saying that Imaginaria is in DANGER!"

Hearing Imaginaria's name, all the evergreens quieted, even Vineous.

I showed them the wand, and their wondrous whispers gave me the courage to speak. "Thank you, Queen," I began. "Let me explain why I know about the white nothingness. The TERRIBLE Witch Violet has used her magic to force Imaginaria to strip all books of their treasures! I am trying to save three of them, so I can bring them back to Imaginaria and free her. But now I realize that I've gotten here too late. I'm sorry!"

Furry began to jump up and down. "Tell me, what great treasure did she take from you? A gem-encrusted CROWN? A valley of golden coins? A tower full of jewels and precious stones? An entire diamond mine?"

I sighed. "Furry, you really are nosy!"

A tear streaked down Roseberry's green cheek. "Nothing of the sort. Witch Violet took our most precious and priceless treasure . . ."

The ferret waited with bated breath — and so did I!

The queen went on.

"Our plant sanctuary disappeared!"

The Plant Sanctuary

"A plant sanctuary?" I asked, confused. "What is that? It sounds beautiful. Is it a kind of greenhouse?"

Sir Vineous looked annoyed. "He's making fun of us! A greenhouse? As if we would ever put our plant friends inside such a prison!"

But the queen stepped in. "Don't speak like that, Cousin. I have read about other worlds where greenhouses are a great *refuge* for some kinds of plants. It allows them to grow in places where they might not have before."

She extended her hand toward a young evergreen, who had delicate skin the color of a seedling. The youngster spoke up. "I am Droplet, the last guardian of the sanctuary. Let me tell you what it's about."

THE PLANT SANCTUARY

"The evergreens are guardians of the plants of our world, a duty that we carry out with care and love. That's why we created the plant sanctuary, a place where seeds of all the plants we know are gathered and preserved. There, they are protected from bad weather and dangerous creatures. The sanctuary is entrusted to a guardian, who protects it."

At the end of her story, Furry's eyes grew wide. "So? That's the whole treasure? I don't get it."

But I understood, and Sophia did, too. "That's just terrible!" she exclaimed. "All the seeds of all the plants, all the biodiversity in your land, is lost?"

Before they could respond, a familiar **buzzing** sound interrupted us.

The paper-eater woodworms had found me and

were DARTING toward us — again!

"Okay, it's been nice, dear evergreens!" Furry cried. "But the moment has come for us to go. Come on, rat, do your little enchanted tumble and let's scram! The treasure's already been all whitened out, anyway! Even if we had found it, it isn't much of a treasure."

But I saw Roseberry's SAD eyes. I couldn't leave her like this! I whispered to Sophia, "I need to speak to the queen. Can you carry me up to her?"

In the flap of a wing, I found myself face-to-face with Roseberry.

"My friend, the woodworms want me," I told her. "If I go, they will leave you alone. But I do believe there is a way for you to have a future here. I would like to stay and try to help you."

The queen looked at me and then at the woodworms, who were heading toward us at full speed. Then she turned to the rest of the evergreens.

"Friends, we will help the Fantastic Hero defeat these enemies!"

Vineous stomped his feet and made everything tremble. "Why should we risk our lives for you?"

But the queen didn't back down. "Not for me,

for the hero! For him, for Imaginaria, and for our **KINGDOM**! We lost our treasure, but we haven't lost our spirit. The evergreen population has never abandoned a living creature who has asked for help, and that will not happen under my reign!"

Roseberry and Vineous looked each other in the eye for a long . . . long . . . long time!

I had to interrupt the face-off. "Your Majesty! The woodworms!"

I pulled out my fantastic pen to shield me from the blow of the first arriving insect.

PHOOOOOOSH!

Vineous's hand hit the woodworm head-on, sending it rolling off into the distance.

"We're with the queen!" Vineous announced. "Let's **protect** the hero!" He turned back to

Roseberry and added, "If this goes badly, it's all your fault!"

The queen took off her crystal CROWN and placed it above Furry, Sophia, and me. Then she explained, "This way, my friends, you'll be safe!"

"No!" I yelled. "Allow us to fight at your side! It's me the woodworms want!"

But she shook her head. "That's right. We're going to protect you!"

That's how the evergreens began a giant battle against the woodworms. Thanks to their size, they managed to keep the insects' attacks at bay. The evergreens hit the woodworms with open hands, as if they were handballs! Cheese and crackers, how strong! But soon, there were so many woodworms that they began to slip through the evergreens' fingers.

Roseberry fought hard. Thanks to her SPEED, she managed to succeed where others had failed.

She moved lightly and silently among the leaves to drive away the woodworms who tried to get to me!

Soon, one of the woodworms managed to sneak through and land right in front of the crystal crown.

I looked at him, and he looked at me.

I saw him open his terrible fangs and thought for sure that he would devour the CROWN.

"It's all over!" Furry yelled. "I'm going to end up woodwormified!"

"Woodwormified?" Sophia retorted. "That's not even a word! What a **ridiculous** end!"

Then, the woodworm let out a strange noise.

"Is it . . . yawning?" I asked in disbelief.

And then, "**BUUURP!**"

Furry muttered, "Is it . . . burping?"

Then the woodworm spoke. "Of course I'm yawning and burping! We ate too much! Witch Violet is making us work too hard. We don't have time to digest or rest! We are tired. Did you know that we usually **sleep** all day? Does it seem right that she's using us this way?"

I was squeakless.

The woodworm continued. "You're the Fantastic Hero, right? We heard that you could help us get some **REST**."

I couldn't believe my ears. "Me? Who told you that?"

"The lady dressed in paper!" the woodworm said simply.

My snout lit up. "Imaginaria! You saw her?"

He shook his head. "No, I didn't see her, but her **words** reached us. Do you think she's someone who we can trust?"

"She definitely is!" I squeaked joyfully.

The woodworm narrowed his eyes at me. "Then help us rest, like she promised!"

Hero's Block

Furry whispered in my ear. "I really didn't expect this!"

That made two of us!

The woodworm came even closer to the crystal wall that separated us and repeated, "Help us! We want to rest!"

"Well," I said, thinking FAST, "have you tried to find a comfortable place to close your eyes?"

The woodworm turned to his companions. "Forget it, this guy is a joke! Let's eat him and get on with it!"

"Nooooo!" I exclaimed, terrified. I tried again. "Tell me, why can't you sleep?"

"Why?" he repeated. "Because we're stressed out, that's why. We're doing too much work!

Our stomachs are full of too much food! We are supposed to capture you, and you're jumping from one book to the next without stopping!"

I really didn't know what to say. I had hero's block!

Sophia **LOOKED** at me. "Think about it. What does the Fantastic Hero do when he wants to sleep?"

I slapped a paw to my forehead. "Of course! I drink chamomile tea!" I exclaimed. "Droplet! You've got some chamomile here, right?"

She nodded. "Of course. We have all plants, possible and impossible!"

I smiled. "Then it's settled. Chamomile tea for everyone!"

In the blink of an eye, Roseberry distributed gallons and gallons of chamomile tea to all the woodworms. At first, they sipped it in confusion, but then they began to look more and more pleased. The tea was working its magic!

Finally, their leader said to me, "We are still in trouble. Witch Violet wants us to follow you everywhere. If we don't **OBEY** her orders, she'll turn us into golden furniture!"

I winked. "Not to worry. For all she knows, you are **FOLLOWING** me. You can use this time to take a nice nap, and when you wake up, you can start looking for me again!"

And with that, the buzzing sounds of the paper-eater woodworms turned into a concert of snores!

"Wahoo!" Furry yelled triumphantly.

Sophia and I jumped on him to keep him quiet.

"Shhhhh, you don't want to wake them, do you?!" I squeaked.

Roseberry laughed quietly as she bent down next to us.

I turned to her. "Now that the woodworms are out of the picture, we need to solve the problem of your missing PLANT SANCTUARY!"

She shook her head. "You should really talk to Sir Vineous. He knows what he is doing, and he will take the crown and —"

"No!" I cried. "I saw your COURAGE! Your kind SPIRIT! I saw how you fought the woodworms, protecting your companions. You can do this!"

Sir Vineous walked up just then. "The hero is right. Maybe I was wrong about you, Cousin."

Roseberry looked at him with wide eyes.

I smiled. "You evergreens have a great team

spirit, and **pure** and loyal **souls**!"

Roseberry shook her head. "Yes, but without our treasure, the future of our world is unclear."

I shook my head. "That's not true! And you haven't given up yet, otherwise we wouldn't be here discussing it."

At that moment, Furry grabbed a cup of piping-hot chamomile tea. "**OUCH!**" he yelled, dropping it to the ground. "I burned my tongue! Is there more?"

I lit up. "Of course, the **ANSWER** is right under our noses! Think about it: You have all the chamomile we needed!"

Roseberry and Vineous looked at me, confused. "So?"

"So, the plants are still all around you, alive and thriving!" I said, excited. "You have all the time you need to rebuild your sanctuary. Divide the tasks, send explorers in all directions, and gather new **seeds**! It's just a matter of working together. Trust me, I've faced a thousand challenges, and I've always gotten through them thanks to the help of my **friends**. It won't be a speedy or easy task, but —"

"It's not going to be impossible, either!" Roseberry concluded, standing proudly. She turned to her people. "Did you hear that, friends? Let's get to work! Our **treasure** is still within our reach!"

The evergreens burst into joyous yells. I looked over at the woodworms, worried, but they kept right on sleeping. Then the celebratory cheers started.

"Hooray for Queen Roseberry!"

I looked at the woodworms again, but luckily they were heavy sleepers. They all just rolled over and kept on snoozing!

I waved to the queen with my paw. "We need to go now—another book awaits us!"

She nodded. "Good luck, friends! And thanks for helping us understand that we should never give up and that there's always a solution if you ask for **help**!"

My heart twirled in happiness. "You're right!"

But she didn't hear me. "What?"

I squeaked at the top of my lungs, "You're right! You should **NEVER** give up — there's always a solution if you ask for help!"

Roseberry looked at me, surprised. "Hero, did you see that the —"

Just then Furry tugged at my sleeve. "Why did you yell so loud? The **woodworms**!"

"Oh, don't worry," I reassured him. "They're heavy sleepers."

But Sophia ruffled her wings, agitated. "You woke them up, cheesebrain!"

Moldy mozzarella, a few woodworms were beginning to open their hungry eyes. **Oh no!**

"We need to go!" I told the evergreens. "See you soon, **friends**! And don't fear the woodworms. As soon as they wake up, they'll come looking for me and leave you alone!"

It was time to perform the **magic** somersault that the Owlets had taught me, yet again.

I clutched the fantastic pen. I began to jump on one paw, waved the pen in the air, and . . . *Go!* I did a **somersault** along with Furry and Sophia. We were really getting good at this! If there were **Fantastic Olympics**, we surely would have had a chance at the gold medal!

As the horizon-page lifted and closed around us, I heard Sir Vineous mutter, "I mean, if you didn't know who that mouse was, you could really take him for a fool."

I didn't have time to respond, because I was

GAME
What book will Geronimo and friends end up in next?
A A math book
B A crossword book
C A book about ogres

You will discover the answers on the following pages!

already in another **fantastic book**! Though, to tell the truth, the atmosphere was very different than the last book.

"Swamp as far as the eye can see!" Furry yelled.

"**YUCK!** Mud everywhere! Double yuck! This place is horrible!" Sophia added.

I wanted to ease the tension, but then I thought about it. "Yes, you're right, it is a horrible place," I agreed. "More than anything, it's gloomy. Brown mud, gray sky, scary clouds. Who knows where we've ended up? Plus, there are swarms of gnats everywhere . . . how

annoying!"

"I think you picked the wrong **BOOK**," Sophia said, rolling her eyes. "Some hero you are. What kind of treasure could we possibly find in a place so deserted?"

"In a place so **HORRIBLE**, you mean,"

Furry said. His voice bounced back to us from somewhere far away.

"Was that you?" Sophia asked, looking frightened. Furry just shook his head, his whiskers **trembling**.

Chunky cheddar, who was that?

Suddenly, the mud beneath us started to bubble.

Moldy mozzarella, we weren't standing on land! We were on the belly of an ogre!

A Thousand and Three-Quarters Ogres

As the gigantic head of that monstrous creature emerged from the mud, the monster sat down and we began to roll down toward his belly button! Squeak!

Too too too toooooooot!

He picked us up with his thumb and pointer finger and dangled us in front of his face. "What strange, rude creatures. How can you say that the Kingdom of a Thousand and Three-Quarters Ogres is horrible?"

Sophia cleared her throat. "To be precise, I never said that!"

Furry pointed to me. "He said it first!"

"That's not true!" I protested.

The ogre thundered, "My kingdom is

terrible! Incredibly monstrous! Amazingly disgusting! Don't you agree?"

We all nodded vigorously. "Of course, King Ogre!"

He filled with pride. "How did you know that I was the king? Because of my size? Because of my smarts?

Because of my stinky, stinky farts?"

I said timidly, "Why, yes, for all those very important reasons. And also because you said that this is your kingdom, so . . ."

He looked at me with admiration. "Oh, I see you're a clever guy — I mean, mouse! What are you doing here, anyway?"

I wanted to think about what kind of answer to give. After all, this was an ogre. He could GOBBLE me up in one bite!

But Furry's tongue was faster than my thoughts. "We're here for treasure! Do you have one?"

"**You!**" the ogre thundered, ruffling my fur with his horribly foul breath. "**It was you!**"

"Uh-oh!" I muttered. "Something tells me that his treasure has already disappeared."

The ogre stood up, furious, still dangling us in the air.

I saw his enormouse mouth open, and I knew that he was about to gobble us up. Yikes!

I had to say something, and fast! "Umm, Sir Ogre, I mean, illustrious King Ogre," I began. "I assure you that we didn't have anything to do with the disappearance of your treasure!"

He froze. "Oh no? If you didn't have anything to do with it, how do you know it's missing? **I didn't tell you that!**"

"Oh boy, he's less of a fool than he looks!" Furry whispered to me.

At this point, I could see all seven of those black ogre teeth up close! I got so close that I came eye-to-eye with an earthworm that had built a nest in there. Gross!

Suddenly, an agitated voice rose from below and distracted the terrible **OGRE**. Whew! "Hey, Stinkley, what are those?"

"An owl, a ferret, and a rat!" another voice said. "Delicacies!"

"Stinkley, you don't plan on eating 'em up all by yourself, do you?"

"Don't you even think about your dearest **friends**?"

I looked down. All around us there were ogres of all shapes and sizes. They all looked different from one another, and each one was scarier than the next!

I stammered,

"HOW MANY OF THEM ARE THERE?"

It turned out that Stinkley of the Putridfords (also called Sludge Heart) was the name of the ogre who was holding us at his mercy. He seemed to forget that he was about to eat us and huffed, "A thousand! I told you that our kingdom is called the **Kingdom of a Thousand and Three-Quarters Ogres**!" He paused. "But I can't take it anymore. They cause such terrible chaos! They always want to eat all together, party all together, and scare the people of the **Unsoiled Soil** all together!"

"But you're the king," Furry said. "Can't you order them to stop and do what you want?"

I shot him a look. "A good king doesn't behave that way, Furry! What kind of advice is that?"

The ogre burst out laughing, still dangling us

dangerously in the air. "Ha, ha, ha! Who told you I'm the king? I'm not the king!"

We exchanged confused glances. "But you said so just earlier!" I squeaked.

Sophia whispered, "It's best not to contradict him!"

Stinkley continued, "Here in the Kingdom of the Thousand and Three-Quarters Ogres, I am just the **HEAD HONCHO**. The king of the Thundering Ogres of All the Most Repugnant Kingdoms said so! His daughter is Princess ***NEVERJOY***. You've heard of her, right?"

Then he sighed, lost in thought. He got so distracted that he totally forgot about us for a moment — and we slipped from his hands!

We fell down, down, down and splatted with a **SPLASHHHH** into the stinky mud.

"They've gotten away!" Stinkley yelled. "My — I mean our — snack! Find them!"

Suddenly, everything erupted into chaos. All the ogres began to run, because all of them wanted to find us first! They began to tumble, fight, and compete. What a mess!

I whispered to my friends, "Quick, Furry, jump on my head! Sophia, fly onto Furry's head! Then let's stick a thousand **swamp algae** pieces on ourselves and cover them up with sticky **MUD**. That way, we can pretend we're an ogre!"

Furry was impressed. "How satisfying! The student — that's you — has learned the art of disguise from the master — that's me!"

In a flash, we transformed into an ogre . . . a very unusual ogre!

An ogre with three heads, ten claws, and two wings!

THE KINGDOM OF A THOUSAND AND THREE-QUARTERS OGRES

The Kingdom of a Thousand and Three-Quarters Ogres is one of the many kingdoms that has fallen under the control of the king of the Thundering Ogres.

It borders the Kingdom of the Grayish Ogres in the north, and the Ever-Evil Ogres in the south. In the east, it borders the Thundering Ogres (home of Princess Neverjoy), and to the west is the Dividing Sea. On the other side of the sea, one can find the Land of Unsoiled Soil, which is inhabited by sweet little ogres who are very careful about their hygiene.

In the Kingdom of a Thousand and Three-Quarters Ogres, there live exactly one thousand ogres, each one different from the next. The "three-quarters" in the name represents the thousands and thousands of teeny-tiny ogres, who are only as tall as three-quarters of an ogre's ear.* There are so many of them that no other kingdom would welcome them. They snuck into this kingdom when Stinkley (also known as Sludge Heart), the head honcho appointed by the king, turned a blind eye. Some say that he did it because his heart is so weak, but the three-quarters say that he did it because his heart is so big. It all depends on your perspective!

*An ogre's ear is a unit of measurement in All the Most Repugnant Kingdoms. They base the measurement on the size of an average-medium ogre, like Stinkley.

"This disguise is terrible!" Furry exclaimed. "I take it back — you're not so great of a student after all!"

Sophia hushed him. "Shhhh! You don't want to attract the ATTENTION of the thousand and three-quarters ogres, do you? What does *three-quarters* mean, anyway?"

Just then a huge ogre yelled at us. "Hey you, did you see those three go this way?"

We were silent.

He looked at us. "You're not going to answer?"

We stayed silent.

He got even closer, suspicious, but then Stinkley yelled, "That's enough! It's your fault that our snack disappeared. Ah well, it doesn't matter, anyway. I have nothing that's worth stuffing myself with, morning or night . . . sigh!"

"Oh no!" exclaimed the massive ogre. "Sludge Heart is whining again!"

Another one jumped in the mud. "Come on, let's hide!"

Furry shrugged. "That's great for us! Come on, hero, do your little **dance** and let's get out of here!"

But I was confused: Those were strange sighs for an ogre! Stinkley seemed worried, hurt, and sad. Why did the others want to run away? I gathered my courage, then I cleared my throat

and asked, "Why is everyone running away?"

An ogre looked at me with surprise. "What kind of a question is that? Where have you been the last two days? Look over there!"

We turned to where he was pointing. Out on the horizon we saw the white nothingness! That enormouse, scary, empty blankness!

"Stinkley had just finished collecting a mountain of gold coins tall enough to satisfy the king of ogres so that he could ask for Princess Neverjoy's hand in marriage. And — POOF! It all suddenly disappeared! Now he's desperate. He says he's in love, but since he isn't noble, the king won't let him marry the princess. If Stinkley doesn't have the gold, he will never agree to let her marry him!"

Then the swamp shook once more. The ogre added, "Oh no, now he's going to start crying! I'm getting out of here!"

A Love Poem

A moment later, enormouse salty drops began to rain down on us! They were Stinkley's **TEARS**! The ogre began to talk to himself.

"To love or not to love?
This is the terrible glitch
of a heart that hurts like a
rash with a swampy itch."

I was stunned. "This is an ogre love poem!"

Sophia cut me off. "Yes, yes, I agree. But can you hurry up? We need to go to another book. There's nothing left to do here!"

But I didn't feel like I could leave. That poor ogre, as **messy** as he was, was sad because of Regulus and Violet's schemes.

What would Imaginaria do if she were there? I couldn't ask her, but I could sense the answer: She would never leave anyone behind!

I looked around to make sure there were no other hungry and gluttonous ogres nearby, then yelled, "Stinkley, tell me about the princess! The treasure is gone, but maybe there is another way!"

The ogre turned toward us, his face wet with tears. "Are you still here? You didn't run off! Do you really want to **help** me?"

Furry and Sophia both said to me under their breath, "You are a fantastic **fool**!"

But Stinkley seemed thrilled that someone wanted to listen to him! He told me every last detail of how he fell in love with the princess of the Thundering Ogres of All the Most Repugnant Kingdoms, and concluded, "She is too good for me! Her father will reject my proposal and it will be all over for me!"

"I don't know if he'll reject you or not," I said, "but what I do know is that you can't think about buying her. Losing the treasure could be a good thing. Now you're forced to make him like you for real!"

Stinkley shook his head. "How can I? I'm just an ordinary ogre!"

"We're all special in different ways!" I exclaimed. "And you write beautiful **love** poems! Did you ever think of reciting them to the princess? Maybe her father will see how much you both love each other and it will change his mind."

Suddenly, the swamp began to shake all around us. The mud began to **boil**! Holey cheese!

"Help! Another fart!" Furry yelled.

Too too tooooooot!

The usual **stench** filled the air. Ugh!

The ogre sighed. "This always happens when I get upset!"

Somewhat dazed from the stench, I squeaked, "So, what were you saying?"

"I can't do it!" Stinkley cried. "I'm a **shy** guy! When I see her, I forget everything I want to say. And I never know what to do with my hands. I'm sure everyone would make fun of me. I mean, think about it. An ogre reciting love poems? Who's ever heard of such a thing?"

I **thought** for a minute. "Let's go to them! The three of us will hide, and I'll give you suggestions for what to say. It will be great!"

Furry smacked his paw against his head. "This won't end well!"

But the ogre seemed to like this plan. He placed us on his enormouse head, behind one ear. "You'll be good here," he exclaimed proudly.

As Stinkley took some huge steps forward, we

began to slip down, down, down his ear, along his greasy skin.

"Grab on to his hair!" I yelled.

But his hair was slippery, too. Who knows when he last washed it!

Luckily, a **GIANT** pimple broke our fall. It was as big as a small hill and poked right up behind the ogre's ear.

At that point, we realized that we must have reached the princess. Sure enough, Stinkley let out another enormouse **fart**!

Too too too-tooooooot!

We struggled to climb

up between one scab and the next. Gosh, this ogre probably hadn't bathed in years, or even centuries! We looked out to see the famouse princess.

She stood right in front of him, and she was looking at him, confused. NEVERJOY was nothing like I expected!

She was, of course, tall and muscular, and her rosy skin was dirty with mud. Her BROWN, lice-ridden hair was twisted into a long braid that wrapped around her head like a crown.

But her eyes were full of joy, which I didn't expect from her name. When she saw Stinkley, she exclaimed, "Stinkley! What are you doing here? My father has been so upset since the treasure disappeared!"

Stinkley was silent. Why didn't he say anything?

Then I remembered. This was why we were here with him!

I **whispered** in his ear. "Tell her that you care a lot about her, and that's why you're here — even if you don't have any treasure."

He repeated, "Tell her that you care a lot about her, and that's why you're here — even if you don't have any treasure."

Princess Neverjoy looked befuddled. "Huh? What are you saying?"

I quickly said, "You don't have to repeat **everything**! Just the things to say to her!"

He continued, "You don't have to —"

But then he stopped. Maybe he had finally understood me!

The ogress, however, was furious. "I don't have to what?"

So I suggested, "Forgive me, light of my eyes, but every time you are in front of me my heart **MELTS** like Brie in the sunshine and my mind falters."

This time, Stinkley repeated everything perfectly — but the princess became even more furious!

"What are you talking about? Why are you talking like that? I don't recognize you anymore! Did you just **invent** the whole story about the treasure going missing because you didn't want to marry me? I can't believe it! To think, I really believed that you were truly **in love** with me!"

That's when I realized the king was hiding in the doorway, listening to every word!

This was going to be easier than I had expected! I said to Stinkley, "Okay, this is it. But you shouldn't use my **words**. Use your own! Tell her one of your poems!"

He muttered, "I don't remember my poems! My mind turns to mush when I'm in front of her. I start to stammer and can't say anything!"

I began to **prompt** him with individual words

of the poem he had told me earlier. He began to repeat the words until he loosened up and could do it himself!

"Through the highs and the lows,
beloved snot of my nose,
adored stench of my toes:
without you I'm lost, that's how it goes!"

The ogress calmed down, and he continued.

"Neverjoy is your name,
but my pain is just the same,
if you won't marry me
as I have asked of thee!"

He stepped forward as the ogress listened in silence. Finally, he was quiet — and I was, too!

Hours had passed! Hours amid all that stench and filth! Furry and Sophia were just as worn out as I was.

Suddenly, Neverjoy whispered, "These poems are **all for me**?"

Stinkley nodded firmly. "All of them! Only for you, my dear princess!"

"So you are in love with me? **Truly?**" she asked him.

"Absolutely, I am!" he bellowed. "But I no longer have a treasure to give you —"

The princess began to laugh. She laughed and laughed, until she ended up on the ground in a fit of laughter. Stinkley was getting **nervous**. I turned to Furry and Sophia. "Hold on tight, there's a fart on the way!"

But then the ogress stood up and wiped her eyes. "Do you know how little I care about that treasure you collected? As if you could really eat **golden coins**!" She ran to hug him. "I'm in love with you, too, silly! This was all a **TEST** from my father! Neither of us care if there is any treasure!"

Furry jumped to his feet. "Oh, good! Are you happy now, Hero? We can go!"

Sophia agreed. "Yes, after this joyous lovefest complete with farts, we can go."

I nodded happily. At that moment, we were lifted up by the ogre's finger.

"My beloved, let me introduce these three, who helped me find the COURAGE to read you my poems!" Stinkley said.

The ogress looked us up and down. "Hmm, a rat, a ferret, and an owl. Interesting! I really could use a snack!"

We Need a Plan!

Meanwhile, back in the Enchanted Library, Violet was leafing through the books around her on the terrace, stressed. "Where did those woodworms end up? Where did that rat go? I must get the wand back at once!"

Imaginaria walked around on tiptoe, PEEKING at the pages of the books the witch was tossing here and there. "You may as well give up. Without my pen, I can't pull any treasures out of the books. If you give me my powers back, I could make the Fantastic Hero return and maybe we could come to an agreement."

"Ha, ha, ha, ha!" Regulus's wicked laugh interrupted her. "Give you your powers back? Dear Imaginaria, you really are in no position to ask for such things."

The Lady of Books responded coldly. "Surely, my position is better than yours!" She pointed to the gray wizard's body, which was still

LEADIFIED.

Violet smiled cruelly. "Exactly, Regulus, you're one to talk! You aren't even lifting a finger to help me! I always have to do everything all by myself. Myself!"

Regulus turned red with anger, but suddenly his face morphed into an evil smile. "That's just because I'm still leadified. If you BURN the books and free me, then I'll be able to help you!"

Imaginaria approached the witch. "Don't believe him! He doesn't think about anyone other than himself, not even you!"

Violet turned slowly toward her and hissed, "Regulus is my love. If anyone here knows him, it's me!"

"Exactly, my dear," Regulus said. "Let's finish our project. *Free me!*"

Violet went to him. "Let's talk about it. You already made me promises in the past . . ."

While those two got into a deep discussion, Imaginaria finally spotted me in

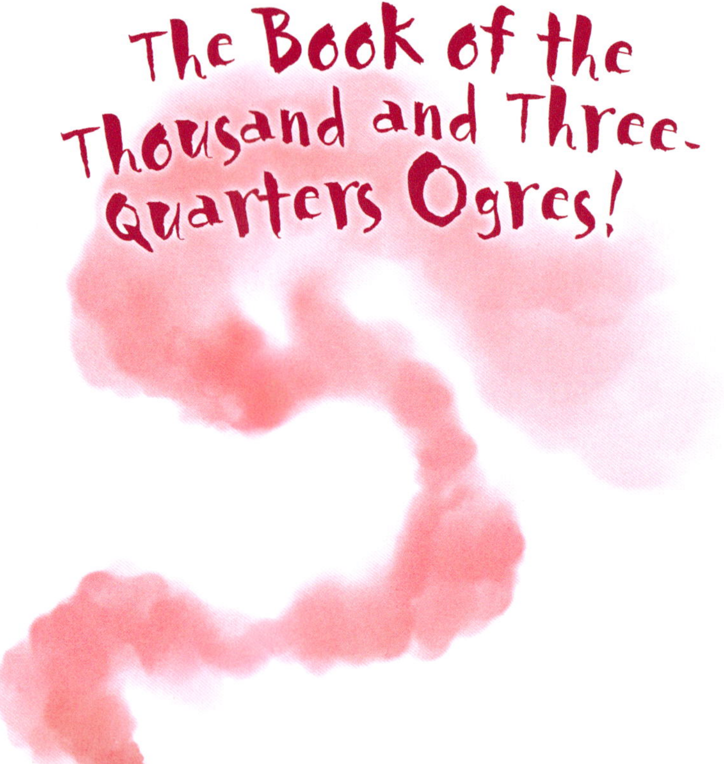

Watch Out!

The ogress was about to eat me up in one bite! Squeak!

But Stinkley stopped her. "No, **my dear** — those creatures helped me! And to tell you the truth, I'm not even sure why."

I jumped in. "**EASY!** I'm the **FANTASTIC HERO**, and I'm here to save Imaginaria. The queen would never leave a fantastic creature in trouble!"

The ogress placed me immediately on her hand. "Wait! You're the **FANTASTIC HERO**? Imaginaria's in trouble?"

I told them everything and then Sophia added, "Anyway, it looks like we got here too late. We're really sorry!"

Stinkley smiled at us. "You know what? I'm

not sorry. It's just like you said, Hero. If the treasure hadn't disappeared, I would never have understood that

true love is worth more than any treasure. It can never be bought!"

Hearing those words, my heart melted like mozzarella cheese. "You're right, my friend!" Then I felt a wave of sadness wash over me. "Unfortunately, that won't help Imaginaria."

The ogress pointed to the **PENDANT** on my neck. "Hero, have you noticed that —"

Just then a familiar buzzing interrupted our conversation. The paper-eater woodworms had arrived!

Where had they come from?

Stinkley and Neverjoy **hollered** and raised their arms to fight off as many insects as possible,

but the woodworms had an advantage. There were so many of them, and the ogres were too big and too slow!

A woodworm plopped down right in front of me. "Ha, ha! Gotcha!"

Before I could **shake** a whisker, he slipped the wand from around my neck.

Oh nooooo!

Then he held it in his mouth and flew up above our heads. This was it! All was lost!

"I will eat them!" Stinkley thundered.

But I put up a paw to stop him. "No, I think there's magic behind this. They're just following Violet's orders."

As soon as the woodworm with the wand

disappeared from sight, the others followed. They weren't interested in us anymore!

I turned to my friends. "They have the magic pen. If they bring it to Violet, all is **LOST**. We need to get back to the Enchanted Library right away!"

"But we don't have the three treasures!" Sophia hooted.

I nodded, saddened. "I know, but we'll just have to find another way to stop her. We need a *diversion* so that we can catch her by surprise! But what could we use to distract her?"

Stinkley smiled. **"A treasure!"**

"Of course!" I cried.

The ogre looked delighted, but then his mood saddened. "But we don't have one."

"But that gave me an idea!" I said.

Free at Last!

While we were being attacked by woodworms and Imaginaria's wand was being stolen, things were still happening back in the Enchanted Library.

"Okay, okay, REGULUS!" Violet huffed. "We will do as you say!"

She began to toss books in the air and reduce them to ashes with her magic.

Imaginaria threw herself on the witch. "No, stop! Don't you see? Regulus is using you!"

In one swift gesture, the witch created a strand of purple chains that wrapped around Imaginaria, binding her. "Ugh, I'm fed up with you. You don't know what you're talking about!"

Violet studied Imaginaria, pleased with her work. "As soon as Regulus is free, he can go into the books and get your magical pen. Then it will all be over for you!"

Meanwhile, Regulus's henchmen were working on the **EVIL** treatments to slowly de-leadify their leader.

Imaginaria watched him anxiously with **TEARS** running down her cheeks. He began to move — first his neck, then a shoulder, then an arm, and finally his legs!

"I'm back!"

Regulus yelled, standing proudly with his terrifying ruler pointed toward the sky!

Violet squealed and gave him an excited hug.

"Good, good, now jump into those books — catch that rat and find my **treasure**!"

But Regulus burst out laughing. "You truly are a fool! I have **NO** intention of going into those fantastic books. I don't care about getting that pen back.

My only goal is to destroy Imaginaria!"

The Lady of Books turned toward the witch. "I'm sorry, but I did warn you! Regulus doesn't care about anyone or anything but himself!"

"How could you do this to me, after I saved you?" The witch let out an angry howl as Regulus raised his powerful RULER at Imaginaria.

Was this the end?

But Regulus hadn't counted on a certain fantastic team! He would be taken by surprise and thrown off his game.

Inside the pages of The Book of a Thousand and Three-Quarters Ogres, my friends and I had finished putting our plan together. We were finally ready to act!

We said good-bye to Stinkley and Neverjoy, and I enacted my magical spell once again. This time, we didn't use it to dive into another book, but to go back to the Tower of Ideas! I just needed to do a backward somersault in perfect sync with Furry and Sophia!

WHOOSH!

The horizon opened once more like the page of a book, and my companions and I were back at the ENCHANTED LIBRARY. We stood up quickly and I shouted,

"The hero has returned!"

For a moment everyone was silent. I had really made a heroic entrance!

But there was no time to celebrate before Regulus burst out laughing. "Ha, ha, ha! You're here, rat, along with those other nothings! It will be a true pleasure to destroy you all together. That way, my revenge will be final!"

I wasn't giving up that easily! I showed him the bag on my back. "Here are the hidden treasures from the books, Imaginaria. I found them! You need to be really careful, because they're super precious."

Regulus snickered. "Do you think I care about those treasures?"

With that, he shot a terrible leadifying ray right at me!

At that moment, the unthinkable happened! Overhearing the promise of treasure, Violet yelled,

"I want them, I want them!"

She quickly diverted Regulus's ray, saving me and shooting it back toward him!

Just like that, Regulus was turned into a **LEAD STATUE**! Again!

"He really never learns!" I muttered under my breath.

Meanwhile, Violet hissed, "That's what you get for making fun of me!"

She was truly pleased with herself! A chill ran down my fur. Once again, the WITCH had proved that she had no honor!

Then I turned to Imaginaria and whispered, "Have the woodworms already brought the wand back?"

She shook her head.

Maybe there was still hope!

But Violet turned toward me. "Give me that bag, mouse!"

It was time to put our **PLAN** into action!

"Of course, you just had to ask," I said sweetly. "Here it is!"

When Violet approached, I gestured to the **Owlets**, who had appeared on the terrace after being called by Imaginaria. They grabbed the bag and flew into the air!

Violet tried to **strike** them with a spell, but Imaginaria said calmly, "Be careful! I mean that

for your sake. You don't want to hit the bag by mistake! What if you **DESTROYED** all the treasures?"

Witch Violet's Real Name

The Owlets passed the bag from beak to beak, keeping Violet occupied.

I walked over to Imaginaria, hanging my snout. "My friend, **forgive** me — I failed you. I let them steal the wand, and I didn't find any treasure."

"Are you serious?" she asked.

AND SHE SMILED AT ME!

How strange!

"Yes, that's right," I said. "To tell you the truth, I thought the woodworms had already come back here to bring Violet the wand."

Suddenly, out of thin air . . .

The woodworm who had stolen the wand appeared out of nowhere!

He still had it between his teeth. "**BURP!** I knew I shouldn't have stopped to eat that page of newspaper. That **INK** isn't sitting well in my stomach!"

Violet noticed him as well. She held her hand out toward him, never taking her eyes off the bag of treasures. "Finally! Hurry up, give it here!"

As soon as she had the wand in her hands, everything would be lost!

But the woodworm didn't give it to her right away!

"You must give it to me!" Violet hollered. "The spell says so, clearly!

"Bring the magic pen to me,
your most dearly beloved lady!
And if this is something you can't complete,
I'll turn you into a golden love seat!"

But the woodworm still hesitated.

Imaginaria looked up at the woodworm and smiled sweetly. "Hi, small and **hungry** woodworm. Do you remember me?"

Meanwhile, the witch had managed to grab the bag.

"I hope we still have a chance," I whispered under my breath, "but if she gets the pen, everything is **lost**!"

Violet untied the rope, then smiled mockingly. "Ahh, finally, new treasures!"

But as soon as she opened the bag, dozens of tiny **OGRES** popped out! They were the famouse three-quarters ogres, all three-quarters of an ogre's ear tall! They were very small . . . but monstrously **MEAN**!

Our plan was working!

The ogres all yelled, "For Stinkley and Neverjoy! For the hero! For Imaginaria!"

They **LAUNCHED** themselves in every direction, causing all sorts of confusion.

"They will buy us some time," I said to Imaginaria, "but we should still hurry. What do we do next?"

Imaginaria grinned at me. "This!"

She turned to the woodworm once more.

"Remember?
Small little creatures involved in this caper,
listen to this lady, dressed all in paper.
I have no powers and no gold anymore,
but all my creatures, even you, I adore!"

Violet threatened the woodworm with a wave of her arm. "Give me the wand! I am your **BELOVED** lady! The spell that I put on you is clear: If you don't obey, you will become a golden love seat!"

The woodworm fluttered about for a moment. Imaginaria winked at him, and he began to nosedive downward. He got right over our heads and let the **wand** drop!

But it didn't fall into the hands of the witch. It fell into Imaginaria's hands instead!

The witch shook with rage. "No! You didn't obey the spell! You and the other woodworms will become **furniture**!"

The woodworm

retorted, "We aren't afraid of you. YOU aren't our beloved lady — **Imaginaria** is! She will keep us safe!

Imaginaria turned to me. "Luckily, the witch made poor word choices for her spell. It left space for **uncertainty**, and I managed to use that to my advantage."

Witch Violet was fuming with rage. "It doesn't matter! You can only use the pen as I say! Remember? You remain powerless! I sucked your powers out by separating you from your beloved **library**!"

I looked at Imaginaria in shock. "It's true, I never found the treasures that could have given you back your strength and energy! I'm so sorry I failed you."

But suddenly, behind me, Furry, Sophia, and the Owlets appeared, followed by the other fantastic characters we had met on our travels!

They were all popping out of books like cheesy popcorn!

There was Lucy with her PIRATES: "We're coming, Hero!

We won't leave you alone!"

The EVERGREENS, led by Roseberry and Sir Vineous:

"We're here! We couldn't go back!"

Stinkley and all the other OGRES:

"You won't get rid of us that easily!"

I looked at them all, moved. I really didn't know what to say!

"Do you see how many treasures you brought me, my hero?" Imaginaria whispered.

Violet cackled. "Perhaps you have all forgotten that Imaginaria is still under my control! I am the strongest one here!"

She lifted her wand to shoot out a PURPLE RAY of magic.

Violet was so focused on her rage, in fact, that she didn't notice that Korax had swooped down and taken the locket she wore around her neck.

My eyes widened and I gasped in surprise. Had I really just seen that?

A voice behind me made me jump. "That witch made a huge mistake leadifying my boss!"

It was Mercutio!

"My boss wants you to know that the witch's real name is written inside her locket," he went on. "Read the name and see what happens!"

I got chills! When I turned around, Mercutio had disappeared and Korax tossed the pendant at me.

I grabbed it in midair, but it was too late. Violet had already shot her purple ray!

Squeak, what a feline fright! Everything seemed to be moving in slow motion!

The ray got closer and closer and closer . . . but suddenly, a wall of golden words appeared before us. The ray broke across the words, like a wave of water on a rocky shore!

Imaginaria had created a shield of words with her wand!

My mouth hung open watching the Lady of Books. She rose between us and Violet, glowing.

"You have your powers back?" I squeaked in disbelief. "How?!"

Crusty cat litter, what a turn of events!

Witch Violet became so filled with RAGE that she began to turn purple and grow bigger and bigger! I didn't see that coming!!

Korax warned me, "You'd better get a move on, rat. When she gets really angry, she explodes!"

I read the name on her locket. "Aridia . . ."

Imaginaria looked at me, then at the locket. In a flash, she understood. She began to repeat,

Violet turned more and more purple — and more and more **huge**!

Then all of us called out her name in unison:

In that moment, the locket sparkled, opened, and sucked Violet up. She was now miniature-sized — and imprisoned inside!

"So she's a shape-shifter, too!" Imaginaria said. "That's how she managed to separate me from my library. Just like all shape-shifters, she knows the art of mutation and used it against me. At that point, it didn't take much for the bewilderment

spell to work. It's best if we seal up the locket before she manages to transform again!"

With a touch of the wand, the locket closed on Violet's **FURIOUS** face.

THE TRUE TREASURE OF BOOKS

Violet had been defeated!

But I still had a question. "Imaginaria, how did you stop that purple ray? I thought you didn't have your magic powers! How did you get them back?"

She smiled. "It wasn't me. You did it, Fantastic Hero! You found the true treasures hidden in the three books. Do you remember?

Three is the golden number
Three is our saving grace
Three treasures from three books
Is all that's sure in this whole place!"

I didn't understand one lick of what she was saying. "But I didn't find any treasure! The treasures had already been taken!"

Imaginaria looked amused. "Think about it: Did you find nothing in those books? Nothing that might light up my wand and make its ***fantastic heart*** happy? Anything that made your heart happy?"

I peered around at the new friends that I had met. "I found fantastic adventures and fantastic friends!"

Imaginaria lifted her arms triumphantly. "That is what counts! You lived those books, Geronimo! And you found three precious treasures:

2 The knowledge that you should never give up and that there is always a solution if you ask for help!

3 The certainty that true love is worth more than any treasure and can never be bought!

"True treasures in books are like that," Imaginaria went on. "Treasures are the hidden worth between their lines, the **adventures** that get carried out in their pages, the characters you meet, the imagination their words ignite! Worth, adventures, and imagination filled my wand — and our hearts! This is what you gave us, dear Geronimo. Thank you, Fantastic Hero!"

I listened in disbelief. All my **friends** gathered around to pat me on the back, to smile at me, or to shake my paw.

"But if you regained your powers," I said, "how are you still separated from the ENCHANTED LIBRARY*?"

"Now that we have been separated once, we can't go back," Imaginaria said sadly. "But our

*Imaginaria is a shape-shifter. When Regulus hit her with a spell in the past, she transformed into the Enchanted Library.

bond will continue forever. This dear library and I have too much in common!"

I was shocked. "So we did it after all? We saved you?"

Imaginaria was about to respond, but another voice cut her off.

"Don't brag too much, Hero! You saved her . . . for now!

I will return, and you won't escape again!"

At the end of the terrace, Korax and Mercutio had lifted leaden Regulus onto their shoulders. This time, they had managed to free his mouth.

"Squeak!" I exclaimed. "It's Regulus!"

Just then Regulus and his henchmen got sucked into the pages of a book! Rats!

"Is he ***ESCAPING***?" I cried.

Imaginaria looked thoughtful. "He had prepared

for everything. I didn't think he'd actually be able to get into the books!"

Sophia flapped her wings. "Come now, Hero, do your spell and let's go capture that rascal!"

"No," Imaginaria interrupted. "If I know Regulus, he will have already disappeared in the creases of the pages. It's useless to drive him out now. Anyway, without the fantastic ashes he will stay leadified forever!"

My whiskers drooped. "Holey cheese balls, we won the battle, but Regulus still managed to escape! And even though I found three treasures and you regained your powers, there's nothing we can do about the BOOKS that were ruined and burned with magic." I hung my snout.

Imaginaria looked at me, a light shining in her eyes. "What is all this gloom, Hero? Do you think I asked you to find the true treasures of the books just to help me? No, my friend, what you brought me is much more precious — we need it to save all the books! Tell me again about your adventures in *The Book of Pirates*, *The Book of the Evergreens*, and *The Book of a Thousand and Three-Quarters Ogres*."

And so, with my heart full of **hope**, I began to tell her. As I spoke, Imaginaria began to twirl, tracing my words in the air with delicate flying **GOLDEN LETTERS** . . .

Instantly, the fantastic ashes that still covered the top of the tower lifted into a luminous vortex.

And in this vortex, there were books that found their pages, pages that found their words, and words that found their letters!

All the fantastic characters dove happily back into their books!

Sophia leafed through pages, unable to contain her joy. "The missing words have returned! This book has risen from the ashes! It's all here!"

Furry trotted up and down the terrace, singing and tossing the books to the **Owlets**. "A book here, a book there, the library will be in order everywhere!"

The Owlets grabbed the books in the air and flew to put them on various shelves, singing, "All's well that ends well!"

I watched them, unable to do anything other than sing along.

The Grand Reception

Only a few hours had passed since Imaginaria had put all the fantastic books back into perfect condition, and I was **exhausted**! Why? Well, because Sophia was making me work my tail off!

"Come on, Fantastic Hero! Don't just loaf about!" she yelled. "Did you think you could just stand there, singing a little? You're as tone deaf as the Complaining Trolls! No, no, no, my dear, we have an Enchanted Library to get in tip-top shape! Tip-top, you hear me? Don't think that your rank as **FANTASTIC HERO** means that you don't have to pitch in! This **mess** is your fault, too!"

"Why does it have to be my fault?" I squeaked.

"Where should I begin?" Furry jumped in.

"**WHO** wasted all that time making the pirates nervous? **WHO** landed us right smack in the house of the Relentless Kraken? **WHO** got the attention of the paper-eater woodworms? **WHO**—"

I held up a paw. "Oh, come on, I didn't do any of that on purpose! It was all part of the mission! You know that!"

But the ferret and the owl started whispering. Squeak, they really could get along, especially when it came to taking things out on me!

Finally, Sophia announced, "We partially accept your observations and declare that you can be excused from the heaviest tasks here in the library!"

I was satisfied. "Now you're talking!"

Furry cut me off. "Also because we're finished here! The library and the books are all in order. Now we have to get everything ready for the

GRAND RECEPTION! And that's up to you, obviously."

I looked up to the sky. Cheese and crackers, would it ever end? "But when can I go back home?"

Just then Imaginaria arrived. Her eyes went wide with surprise. "Oh, friends, what a beautiful job you've done! How marvelous!"

Furry and Sophia both stood up tall. "Thank you, our lady! Everything will be even more marvelous tonight!"

The owl adjusted her glasses and began to read me the list of things to do. "Before all the guests arrive, you must prepare fifty-seven tables of eighteen seats each — not one more, not one LESS! Then you must arrange 1,026 chairs, 3,078 plates and glasses, and don't forget the silverware!"

My fur turned white. "But that's so many things!"

Furry shrugged. "Oh, this is just what you have to do in the **GREAT HALL**. Then there are the other thirty-five rooms and the three gardens. Mouse, you don't really think that we could fit all the ogres in here, do you? And the giants? Have you even thought about all the dragons? You will have to deep clean the infinite fountain, otherwise where will we put the **RELENTLESS KRAKEN**? By the way, it sounds like he complained about your little joke with the pepper. I warned you he wouldn't find it funny."

I was about to faint, but luckily Imaginaria stepped in.

She burst out laughing. "There's no **TIME** for all of that!" She turned and spread her arms. "The guests are already arriving!"

One by one, like popping kernels of popcorn, they all appeared —

thousands and thousands and thousands of fantastic characters!

Imaginaria twirled from one character to the next like the perfect hostess. Banquet tables and colorful **decorations** popped up here and there, thanks to her wand.

I looked sideways at Furry and Sophia. "Could I have fixed the Enchanted Library with the help of my ***fantastic pen***?"

They shrugged, but I was quickly distracted because I saw Neverjoy and Stinkley, Vineous and Roseberry, Lucy the Fearsome, and the Three-Quarters Ogres arrive!

Then so many dear friends that I had met in the past appeared.

How fantastically fabumouse to see them all again!

Each one of them had something to tell me, and I was happy to chat with them all!

As my friends filed up one after another, I heard a unicorn ask Furry, "Excuse me, but can you tell me how to get to my book? Could you help send me home? I forgot **Imaginaria's** present!"

"But of course!" Furry said. "No problem. Am I or am I not the

fantastic helper?"

I've never seen him so happy as when he was able to help the unicorn make its way back home!

Then I saw a small elf pull on his dad's jacket. "Daddy, can we go home? I'm tired!"

I smiled at the request, and suddenly I felt something in my heart. I was **homesick**, too!

The moment had come for me to say good-bye to Imaginaria. As I thought it, she appeared before me, smiling **sweetly**.

"It's time for me to go home now," I said. "My family and my friends must be worried! I have to go reassure the Golden Card, too. Who knows how it feels, all **alone** in my office?"

Imaginaria winked at me. "Don't worry, Geronimo, time in New Mouse City passes differently."

With a wave of her hand, she made my beloved Golden Card appear in front of me.

I couldn't believe my eyes!

The card rubbed up against my snout **affectionately** and then slipped into my pocket. I looked at Imaginaria in awe. "You always think of everything, don't you?"

She **hugged** me. "I try. But I'm lucky — I have many friends to support me. Thank you for being one of them, my **FANTASTIC HERO**!"

I headed toward the door of the Enchanted Library, smiling at the memory of the first time I had gone through that door and entered that magical world. This time, I was leaving that world behind as I stepped paw back in New Mouse City!

As the door of the building closed behind me, I

was once again in **Singing Stone Plaza**.

I looked at where Regulus's statue had been just a short while ago, and I got chills. Maybe one day the wizard would return! But if he did, I was sure that I could face him with my fantastic friends.

I began to **WALK** down the streets of the city that I loved. They were so familiar and so magical at the same time. As I looked around with a full heart, I sighed happily. "Once again, I learned something new and precious about the **power of books** . . .

"And that's a promise, or my name isn't Stilton,

Geronimo Stilton!"

DON'T MISS
GERONIMO'S
LAST ADVENTURE

The Hero's Dream

One evening, I was wandering the streets of New Mouse City, feeling confused. Everything was covered in this **STRANGE**, ink-like **darkness**. It seemed almost magical. I wandered through the dark and tried to figure out exactly where I was. Holey cheese! How could I be lost? I knew New Mouse City like the back of my paws!

It seemed like I was wandering through a dream I had been having over and over again all week. It was always the same: I walked and walked without knowing where I was going. The story repeated, and the whole time, I thought I heard my name **echoing** in the distance.

"Geronimo . . . Geronimo . . . Geronimo . . ."

I perked up my ears to listen more closely.

"Stilton . . . Stilton . . . Stilton!"

Suddenly, I found myself in **Singing Stone Plaza**. Before me stood an ancient building.

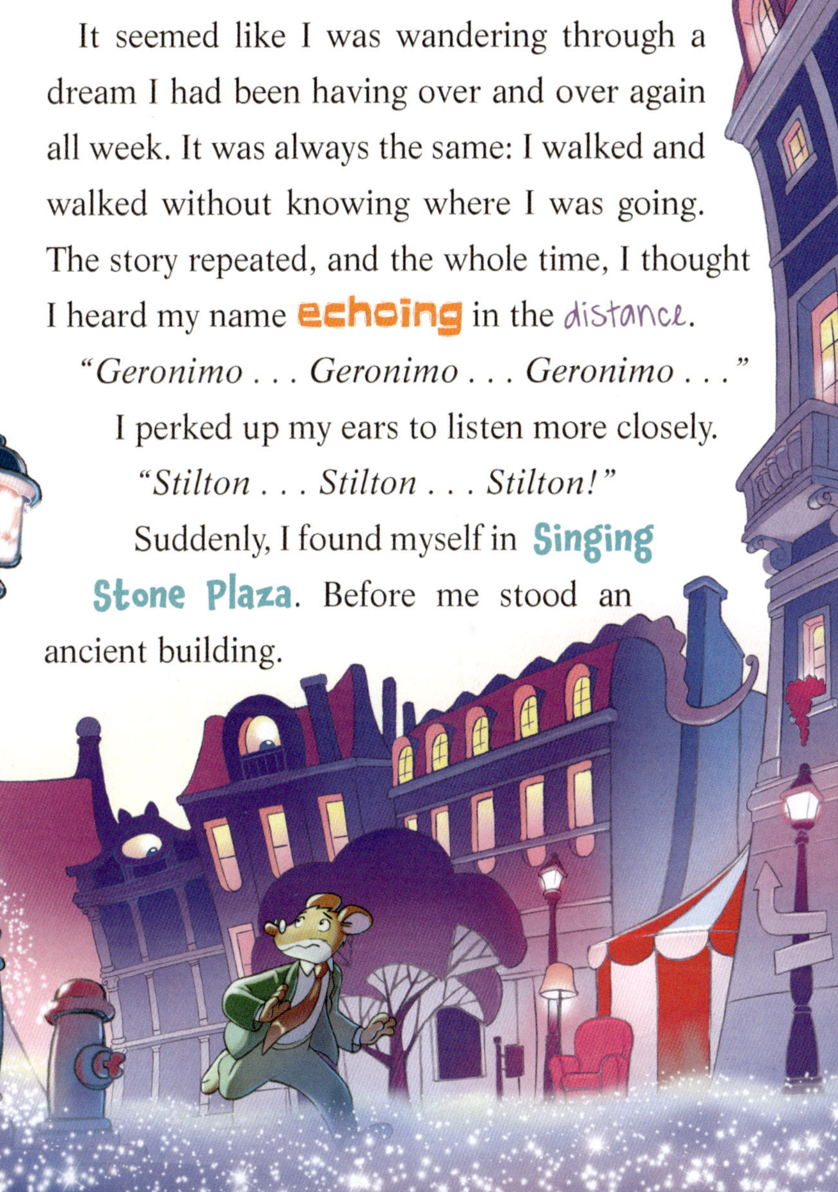

I knew this place well! I had passed it many times before, but I remembered it dilapidated and crumbling. Now it was so beautiful — each detail was perfect!

At the entrance stood a golden stand, and above the door there was a strange **SUNDIAL**.

Just then I realized that the mysterious voice that seemed to be calling me was coming from inside the building! I tiptoed closer on trembling paws and noticed that the door was slightly open.

"Squeeeeak!"

My voice echoed in the silence and scared me out of my fur! Moldy mozzarella!

I ducked through the doorway and tried to hide inside the building, but . . . a ***whirlwind of golden sparkles*** blocked my path!

After a moment, it vanished. In its place was a woman, wearing a magnificent dress made of

thousands of paper pages filled with sparkly writing. She held what looked like a precious golden pen. But the most remarkable thing about her was her sweet smile!

Her voice was also **sweet**. "Oh, my hero, I finally found you! You're fantastic, just like I *imagined*!"

I stepped back. Me? A hero?

The woman must have seen the confused look on my snout. "You are the only one who can save me. You must accept!"

I was so shocked I could barely squeak! "Um . . . accept? Accept what?"

She waved her golden pen as if casting a spell. We suddenly found ourselves in an enormouse room. It had a high ceiling decorated with detailed murals. The woman in front of me was the same as the face in the paintings, too! But before I could look at anything else, the walls filled with shelves and shelves of all types of **BOOKS**.

For the love of cheese! Thousands and thousands of volumes flew here and there. They all seemed to be moving in a very specific order.

"This is a library?" I asked in awe.

The woman smiled.

*"Look around; what you see is true.
This is the enchanted space
that I have conjured just for you."*

I looked around dreamily. "Where are we?"

She didn't answer my question. "My name is Imaginaria, and I need your help! You're about to become a Fantastic Hero."

I twisted my tail into a knot. "Me?! I think you've got the wrong rodent. My name is *Stilton*, *Geronimo Stilton*. I'm not a Fantastic Hero!"

"You are the **defender**, the Fantastic Hero — you just don't know it yet!" Imaginaria said kindly. "My words seem mysterious now, but soon you will understand. First, you need to enter the library with the **KEY**."

"The key?" I asked, more confused than ever. "What key?"

Imaginaria smiled. "You will find the key where you seek it to be. Follow the card that will appear; believe me, it will serve you here!"

Chattering cheese puffs, I had no idea what she was squeaking about now! "The **CARD**? What card?"

Imaginaria laughed. "You'll need an enchanted card for the

Then she opened her arms and began to spin, filling the room with a thousand golden sparkles.

My head began to spin, too, and I felt my paws turn as limp as string cheese. Just then, I heard the beat of a pendulum.

Dong, dong, dong!
Dong, dong, dong!
Dong, dong, dong!

My eyes flew open. It was exactly midnight! And I wasn't in the library — I was in my bed, in my own home!

Holey cheese balls, it was all just a **dream**!

How strange. I'd been having this same dream for a week now!

I glanced over at my nightstand, and there, just as Imaginaria had warned me, I saw the sparkly golden card.

"So it wasn't a dream?" I yelped.

I grabbed the card with my paws. It was real!

I read the writing: ENCHANTED LIBRARY.

It even had my picture, my name, and my address on it. Squeak! Now what was I supposed to do?

A Night in New Mouse City

At that moment, the card that I was holding in my paws began to vibrate.

"Thundering cat tails," I squeaked to myself.

The whole thing had really happened.

My dream had become reality!

Why, oh why, do these things always happen to me?!

There were only two things I could be sure of: that I was in my house, and that it was midnight. I racked my brain, trying to remember what Imaginaria had said to me in the dream.

She had called me a hero!

And even FANTASTIC! Me? No way!

She said that I was a defender . . . but a defender

of who or what? Cheese niblets, maybe I should have asked! Now it was too late. I was such a cheesebrain!

Even though I was confused and scared out of my fur, I decided that I had to find out more.

Then I got an idea: I needed to fall back asleep! Then I would go back to dreaming, Imaginaria would reappear, and I could ask her all my questions. This time, I would ask the right ones!

I slipped under the covers and closed my eyes, but I was too worked up to sleep.

So I got up and made myself a gallon of triple-chamomile tea. It was so relaxing!

Next, I tried to **meditate**. I sat with my paws crossed and closed my eyes, trying to clear my head. What peace, what tranquility, what sleepiness! I was almost . . .

BOOM!

Crusty cat litter, something struck me right in the snout! I squeaked in fear and opened my eyes. Flying in front of me was the golden card! Had the card really flown through the air and hit me? How was that possible?

That was something else I could have asked Imaginaria — if only that card would let me get back to sleep! Instead, the more I tried to shoo it away with

my paw, the harder it tried to fly right back at my snout.

Finally, I cried, "**Come on, why won't you let me be?**"

In response, the card flew toward the door, turned around, and flicked my undertail! I yelped. "You aren't trying to tell me that I need to leave the house at this hour, are you?"

The card **JERKED** forward and began to jump back and forth between me and the door over and over again. I sighed and rubbed my eyes. "Cheese and crackers, am I really listening to an enchanted library card?"

Resigned to my fate, I decided to get dressed. Then I headed to the kitchen to grab a quick **snack**. I would need all the energy I could get!

At that moment, the card blocked my way!

"Oh, come on now," I said. "Don't be a bully!"

But the card didn't move. I tried to speak with

it frankly. "Listen, I'm the **BOSS** around here. I won't let a library card tell me what to do. Do we understand each other? Now, I am going to go and have a snack, whether you like it or not!"

The card moved aside. Whew!

I was about to open the refrigerator when the card began to SWIRL around me, flying superfast.

Squeak! I began to spin like a top, too. My poor stomach! "All right, no snack, I promise! I'll leave now!" I yelped.

As soon as those words had left my mouth, the card relaxed. As I headed out the front door, it slipped into my jacket pocket, safe and sound.

I could have sworn I heard the card breathe a sigh of relief!

I walked down the streets of *New Mouse City*. My city was fast asleep.

I clutched at my jacket and peered up at the sky.

"This night is so dark . . ."

I took a deep breath, gathered my courage, and headed toward Singing Stone Plaza, in the **oldest** part of the city.

As I walked, I began to get a strange feeling. It seemed like the silence around me was thicker and heavier than usual. For a moment, I thought I could see **golden sparkles** floating in the air in the distance, just like I had in my dream. Was it possible?

Maybe Imaginaria had sent them to show me the way. Or maybe it was just my imagination.

I shrugged my shoulders and continued.

But something strange was going on . . .

"Beware the cat and the crow!" a little voice next to me whispered.

I jumped and turned, but no one was there — except the picture of a winking rodent on an advertisement!

For a moment, it seemed like the rodent really moved!

Then I heard a **SOUND** behind me. Rat-munching rattlesnakes! But when I turned, I didn't see anyone, so I continued on. I couldn't shake the strange feeling that something was watching me.

Was someone following me?

I turned around again and thought I saw a shadow duck behind a streetlamp. I squinted to get a better look, but the streetlamp went out! Then the red traffic light next to it began to blink, almost like it was warning me of danger! Another shadow darted through the darkness.

I began to run as fast as my paws would take me, until I arrived on the outskirts of the park.

Panicked, I squeaked, "**Run, save yourselves!!!**"

I was about to turn down a path into the park

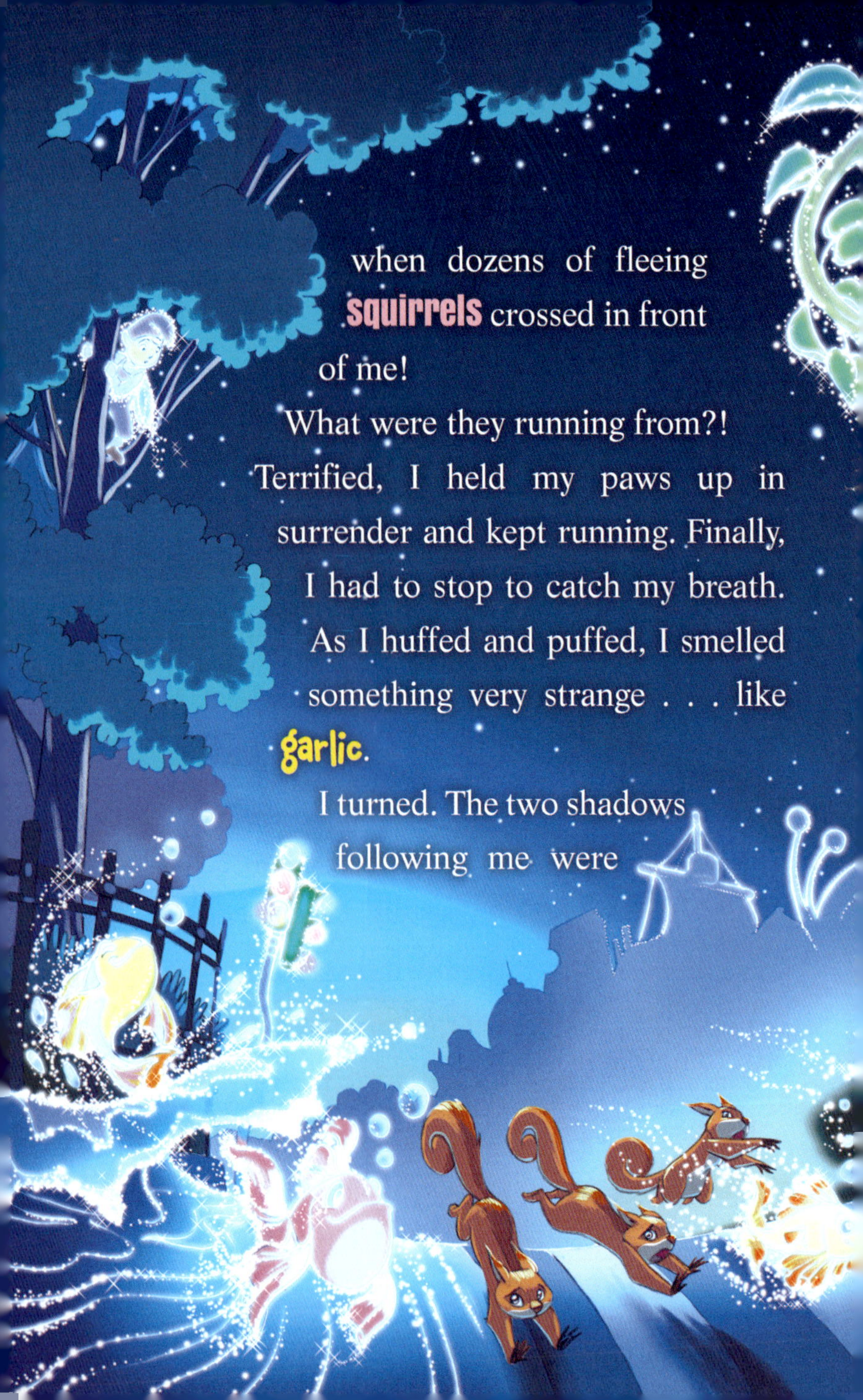

when dozens of fleeing **squirrels** crossed in front of me!

What were they running from?!

Terrified, I held my paws up in surrender and kept running. Finally, I had to stop to catch my breath. As I huffed and puffed, I smelled something very strange . . . like **garlic**.

I turned. The two shadows following me were

getting closer and closer. The traffic lights and streetlamps began blinking again!

WHAT A FELINE FRIGHT!

A Sparkly Golden Key

I was about to pinch myself, but suddenly I could see who had been following me. It was an enormouse **CAT**.

And he was pointing right at me while he **licked his whiskers**!

Squeeeeeeeak! I'm too fond of my fur!

The cat was carrying a bag that had a pan, a fork, and a book entitled *One Thousand Ways to Cook a Mouse without Oil* poking out of the top. The smell of garlic grew stronger, and I realized that it was coming from the cat!

How much garlic had he eaten?! And who was the **shadowy figure** next to him?

Chattering cheddar, I was really in over my ears!

In the dark, I could see that the other figure was wrapped in a dark cloak. Instead of walking, he kind of **HOPPED**. How strange!

The cat meowed. "Yum! Who would have thought that the Fantastic Hero would be a good ol' dirty rat?"

He raised an eyebrow. "Plus, he has the golden card. There's no doubt, it's really him."

Don't miss any of my adventures in the Kingdom of Fantasy!

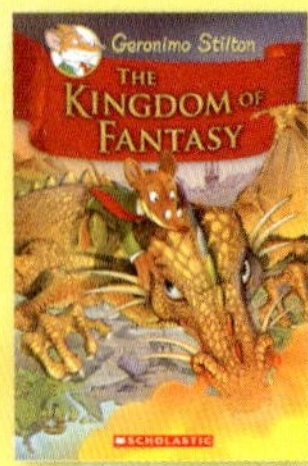

THE KINGDOM OF FANTASY

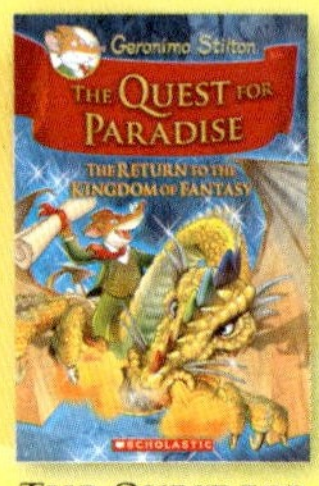

THE QUEST FOR PARADISE:
THE RETURN TO THE KINGDOM OF FANTASY

THE AMAZING VOYAGE:
THE THIRD ADVENTUR IN THE KINGDOM OF FANTASY

THE DRAGON PROPHECY:
THE FOURTH ADVENTURE IN THE KINGDOM OF FANTASY

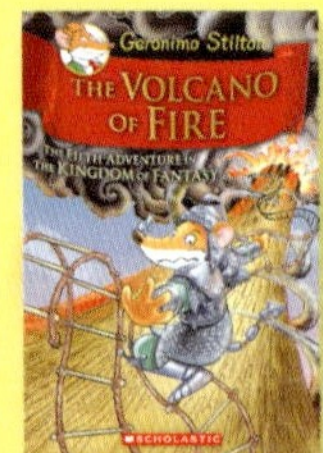

THE VOLCANO OF FIRE:
THE FIFTH ADVENTURE IN THE KINGDOM OF FANTASY

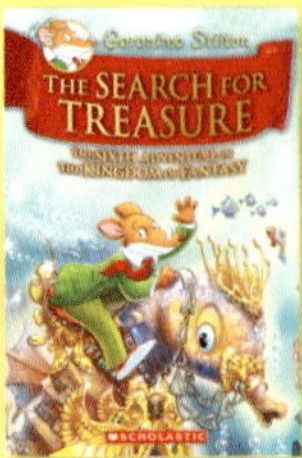

THE SEARCH FOR TREASURE:
THE SIXTH ADVENTURE IN THE KINGDOM OF FANTASY

THE ENCHANTED CHARMS:
THE SEVENTH ADVENTURE IN THE KINGDOM OF FANTASY

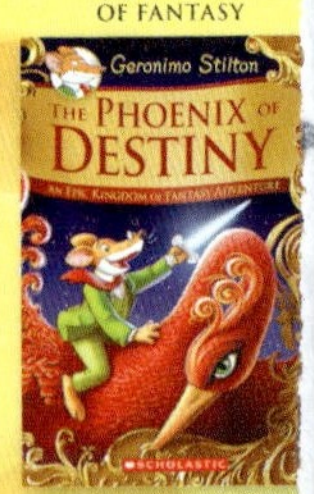

THE PHOENIX OF DESTINY:
AN EPIC KINGDOM C FANTASY ADVENTUR

THE HOUR OF MAGIC:
THE EIGHTH ADVENTURE IN THE KINGDOM OF FANTASY

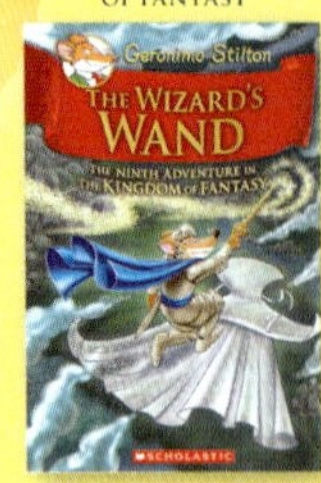

THE WIZARD'S WAND:
THE NINTH ADVENTURE IN THE KINGDOM OF FANTASY

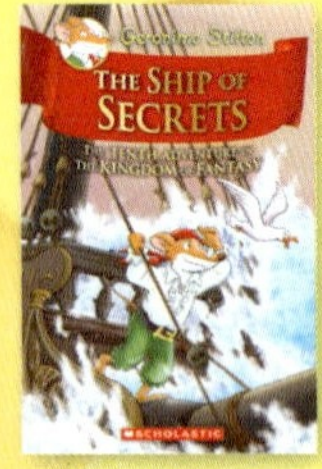

THE SHIP OF SECRETS:
THE TENTH ADVENTURE IN THE KINGDOM OF FANTASY

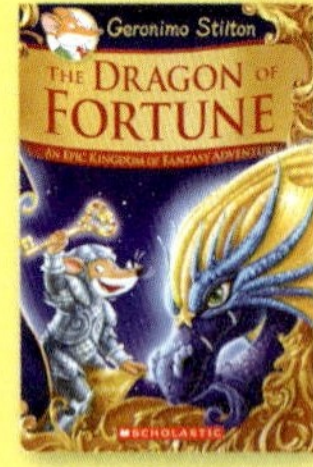

THE DRAGON OF FORTUNE:
AN EPIC KINGDOM OF FANTASY ADVENTURE

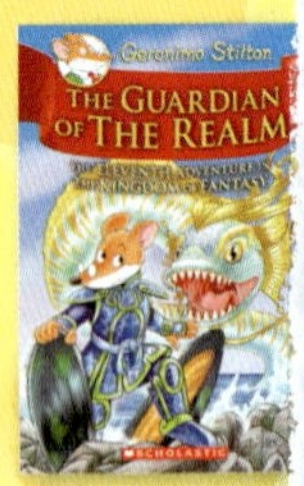

THE GUARDIA OF THE REALM
THE ELEVENTH ADVENTURE IN TH KINGDOM OF FANTA

THE ISLAND OF DRAGONS:
THE TWELFTH ADVENTURE IN THE KINGDOM OF FANTASY

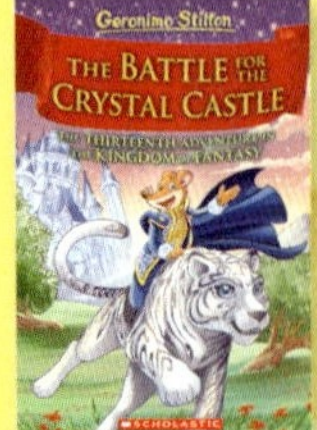

THE BATTLE FOR THE CRYSTAL CASTLE:
THE THIRTEENTH ADVENTURE IN THE KINGDOM OF FANTASY

THE KEEPERS OF THE EMPIRE:
THE FOURTEENTH ADVENTURE IN THE KINGDOM OF FANTASY

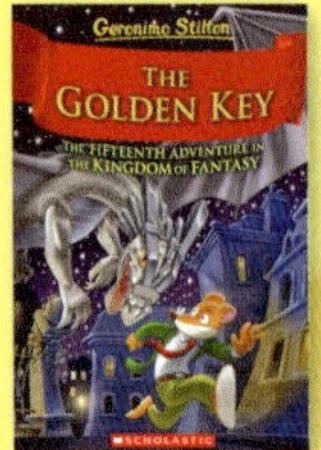

THE GOLDEN KEY
THE FIFTEENTH ADVENTURE IN THE KINGDOM OF FANTASY

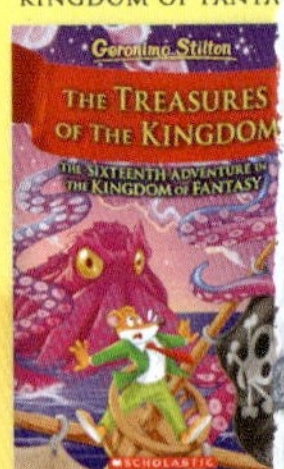

THE TREASURES THE KINGDO
THE SIXTEENTH ADVENTURE IN TH KINGDOM OF FANT